advanced praise for *literary yoga*

Yuriy Tarnawsky's *Literary Yoga* is essential reading by an essential author for anyone interested in engineering the possibility spaces inherent in poetry, prose, and drama through an approach at once methodical, practical, wise, expansive, clear, illuminating, challenging, and, most of all, unfailingly engaging and fun.

—Lance Olsen, author of *Architectures of Possibility: After Innovative Fiction*

Yuriy Tarnawsky has, in *Literary Yoga*, collected a treasure trove of exercises that will help develop the skills of any creative writer, whether experienced or new to the craft. He takes lotus blossoms and opens them up, turns them inside out, and examines them from multiple perspectives. He challenges writers to make conscientious decisions about how to shape their work. How we say what we say changes what we mean, and his demonstrations here are thorough and convincing. This is, simply, the best book of literary exercises since Queneau's famous *Exercises in Style*. *Literary Yoga* deserves a place in writing classes everywhere.

—Eckhard Gerdes, author of *White Bungalows* and *How to Read*

More than any other how-to book for writers that I've read, Yuriy Tarnawsky's *Literary Yoga* nurtures the writerly corpus callosum, connecting craft to creativity. Bi-hemispheric in its construction, with the first half consisting solely of exercises that are simultaneously rigorous and meditative, the second comprised of Tarnawsky's masterly literary demonstrations and commentary, this is a book that acknowledges both left and right brain and promotes their blissful union. Like the eastern physio-spiritual practice that is its namesake, *Literary Yoga* engages the whole of the writer's self.

—Elisabeth Sheffield, author of *Helen Keller Really Lived* and *Gone*

Poems with the narrative drive of a novel; novels with the focus of a poem; and drama as embodied language—these are just three of the connections made throughout Yuriy Tarnawsky's *Literary Yoga*. Unlike most "cookbook" approaches to writing, *Literary Yoga* is an aide to discovery, a compendium of daily exercises that will expand perception and cognition, and yes, even the spiritual aspects of writing as an art form.

—Steve Tomasula, author of *Once Human: Stories*

yuriy tarnawsky

literary yoga

exercises for those who can write

2018

yuriy tarnawsky

literary yoga

exercises for those who can write

Journal of Experimental Fiction 76

JEF Books/Depth Charge Publishing
Aurora, Illinois

Cover Art & Design by Norman Conquest
Author Photo by Oleh Holovackiy

ISBN 1-884097-76-6
ISBN-10 978-1884097-76-8

ISSN 1084-547X

JEF Books/Depth Charge Publishing
The Foremost in Innovative Fiction
experimentalfiction.com

JEF Books are distributed to the trade by SPD:
Small Press Distribution and to the academic
journal market by EBSCO

table of contents

0. introduction

These exercises are designed to improve a person's writing skills. As even a cursory look at them shows, they are purely technical in nature, their aim being to bring to the student's attention the most crucial issues with which the writer is faced in his/her work and to show some of the ways in which they may be tackled. They make the student aware of the choices at his/her disposal.

Although conceived as a textbook, to be used with the help of an instructor, an expert in the art of writing, the book may also be used as a self-study manual by a person who wants to learn writing on his/her own or to hone his/her already proven skills.

The exercises are divided into three independent sections—poetry, prose, and drama. Nominally speaking, therefore, the student may perform only the exercises in the section he/she is interested in and, when doing more than one section, in the order desired. By doing this, however, he/she is bound to diminish the effect the book is intended to have. Due to the nature of literature, the three groups are inextricably linked with each other and form an organic whole. Poetry cannot be practiced effectively without the knowledge of much of the technique of writing prose; good prose cannot be written without incorporating poetic elements in it; and drama is nothing more than prose constrained by time and space. It is strongly suggested, therefore, that the student carries out the three groups of exercises, moreover in their totality and in the indicated order. It is also suggested that if the student is not able to perform all the exercises in the book to his/her full satisfaction and pleasure, it should be taken as a hint that he/she should not try to be a writer. Writing is a lonely and frustrating craft and the student should be grateful he/she has found a way to steer himself/herself away from it.

The book is divided into two parts—the exercises alone, and the exercises with sample texts which illustrate the nature of the tasks assigned to the student. It is up to the student to decide whether he/she wants to do the exercises first and then study the samples, or the other way around.

part one

exercises

1. poetry

The aim of these exercises is to develop the technique of writing free verse. Here then, unless otherwise stated, the word "poem" is understand to mean a free verse poem.

1.1 nature of a poem

The aim of these exercises is to show the nature of the free verse technique—the freedom it gives the poet to express what drives him/her to write a poem.

1.1.1 Rewrite a well-known traditional poem, for instance one of   Shakespeare's sonnets, in free verse, breaking it up into separate lines as your intuition tells you.

1.1.2 Expand the poem from 1.1.1 by adding to it your own   associations, making changes in the original without abandoning the original structure.

1.1.3 Trim the poem from 1.1.2 to its most essential elements, strengthening it by the means that free verse puts at your disposal.

1.1.4 Write your own poem on the same subject as the one in 1.1.1, departing from it as much as you want and utilizing to the utmost the means the free verse technique puts at your disposal.

Compare these four poems. What can you say about them?

Take another well-known classical poem and repeat the exercises.

1.1.5 Rewrite a short prose text—e.g., a passage from a newspaper article, a physics textbook, a cookbook, etc. —in free verse, breaking it up into lines as your intuition tells you.

1.1.6 Expand the poem from 1.1.5 with your own associations as in 1.1.2.

1.1.7 Shorten the poem from 1.1.6 to its most essential elements.

Compare the original and these two poems. Compare them to the four previous poems. What can you say about them?

Take another prose text and repeat the exercises.

1.2 structure of a poem

The aim of these poems is to show the importance of breaking up the text of a poem into lines.

1.2.1 Break up a well-known free verse poem into lines different from the original, adhering to the logic of the contents as your intuition tells you.

(Here every line will constitute an autonomous meaningful unit.)

1.2.2 Break up the poem from 1.2.1 into lines which sometimes violate the logic of the contents. (Here some lines will not constitute autonomous meaningful units.)

1.2.3 Break up the poem from 1.2.2 further into lines which violate the logic of the contents, breaking up individual words where the effect is interesting. (Here still more lines will not constitute autonomous meaningful units.)

1.2.4 Rewrite the poem from 1.2.1 as prose. Now it will constitute a single line.

Compare these five poems. What can you say about them?

1.3 description

The aim of these exercises is to develop the technique of the treatment of poetic subject matter.

1.3.1 Write a poem dealing with a traditional "poetic" subject matter or object—for instance a rose, stars, autumn, etc.— referring openly to its features.

1.3.2 Write a poem on the same subject without

using the words that openly describe it.

1.3.3 Write a poem on the same subject, using words which are in some way opposite to these words, for instance, meat, numbers, a geometric figure in the case of the examples mentioned above.

Compare these three poems. What can you say about them?

1.3.4 Write a poem in the first person singular ("I") about the person.

1.3.5 Rewrite the poem from 1.3.4 in the third person singular ("he/she"), modifying it as needed. If no modification other than pronoun substitution is needed, rewrite the poem from 1.3.4 so that such changes would be needed.

Compare these two poems. What can you say about them?

1.3.6 Write a poem describing an object, for instance an apple.

1.3.7 Write a poem describing the same object as it sees itself.

Compare these two poems. What can you say about them?

1.3.8 Write a poem dealing with an event (action) in the present tense.

1.3.9 Write a poem dealing with the same event in the past tense, making changes when necessary.

1.3.10 Write a poem dealing with the same event in the future tense, making changes when necessary.

Compare these three poems. What can you say about them?

1.4 poetic image

The aim of these exercises is to develop the technique of creating poetic image and stimulating imagination.

1.4.1 Create an unusual simile, for instance, "Water like a hump on a person's back."

1.4.2 Create a construction with an epithet corresponding to the simile in 1.4.1, for instance, "Hunchbacked water."

1.4.3 Create a metaphor in the form "noun phrase 1 of noun phrase 2" that corresponds to the simile in 1.4.1, for instance, "The hump of water."

1.4.4 What images do these constructions evoke in your mind? For instance, "Water looking like a hunchbacked person. The hunchback of water. Deformed water. A hunchbacked sea. The hump of the sea. Water on crutches. The sea on crutches." and so forth.

1.4.5 What opposite images do these constructions evoke in your mind? For instance, "Slender water. A slender sea. Water looking like a princess. The young prince of the sea." and so forth.

Permute the order of the above exercises and go through the specified steps. Repeat the exercise a few times.

1.4.6 Create an image based on a compound noun construction, e.g., "A cloud is a skybruise." List associated images the image evokes, e.g., "A bruised sky. The sky beaten black and blue. The sky has been in a bad fight."

1.4.7 Describe in a few words an object or a phenomenon, then create a poetic image of it as it pops into your head and proceed improving the image until you feel it has reached its full potential, e.g., "A red comet in the night sky. A comet blazing through the night sky, its red tail trailing behind it. A comet blazing through the night sky, its red hair streaming behind it. A mad comet speeding through the night sky, its long red hair streaming behind it. A mad comet speeding naked through the night sky, its long red hair streaming behind it."

1.4.8 Create a compact poetic image (metaphor, simile, etc.) and expand it into a description with the original image at its core, e.g., "Fists of clouds. Clouds rioting above the city, their angry fists raised high."

1.4.9 Create a few original puns.

How do they compare to metaphors and other tropes?

2. prose

The aim of these exercises is to develop the technique of writing fiction (but see 2.7.12 below).

The tasks spelled out in the exercises below connected with texts, unless otherwise noted, refer to narrations, that is, should constitute descriptions of objects or actions and be roughly between 100 and 500 words long.

2.1 language

The aim of these exercises is to show the influence of language on a work of fiction.

2.1.1 syntax

These exercises concentrate on the field of syntax. They show the influence of syntax on a work of fiction.

2.1.1.1 Write a text in what you consider to be your "normal" language.

2.1.1.2 Rewrite the text from 2.1.1.1, eliminating compound sentences and making changes when necessary.

2.1.1.3 Rewrite the text from 2.1.1.2, eliminating

subordinate clauses and making changes when necessary.

2.1.1.4 Rewrite the text from 2.1.1.3, replacing noun modifiers and similar constructions with simple sentences, wherever possible, making changes when necessary.

2.1.1.5 Rewrite the text from 2.1.1.4, introducing into it compound sentences, subordinate clauses, and conjunctions only where this is necessary, to make it more natural.

Compare these five texts. What is the difference between them? What general conclusions would you draw from the texts? What distinguishes the text in 2.1.1.4 from that in 2.1.1.5?

2.1.1.6 Rewrite the text from 2.1.1.1 as one sentence, making changes when necessary.

Compare these six texts. What distinguishes the text in 2.1.1.6 from the preceding ones?

2.1.1.7 Write what you consider to be a stream of consciousness text, that is, a text that is defined as internal monologue that describes the process going on in a mind in which external information is intermixed with internally engendered thoughts.

What can you say about the text in 2.1.1.7? How does it compare with the text in 2.1.1.6?

2.1.2 punctuation

The aim of these exercises is to show the influence of punctuation on a work of fiction.

2.1.2.1 Rewrite the text from 2.1.1.6 without punctuation marks, making changes when necessary to make it better understandable.

How does the text in 2.1.2.1 compare with the text in 2.1.1.6?

2.1.2.2 Rewrite the text from 2.1.2.1 with punctuation marks, inserting them at times in different places from those in the text in 2.1.1.1, in order to change its effect or meaning. If the text in 2.1.2.1 is not amenable to this, write another text and do the exercise with it.

What can you say about this text? Does it have any practical value?

2.1.2.3 Rewrite the text from 2.1.2.1 with punctuation marks, inserting them at times in different places from those in the text in 2.1.1.1, in order to give it an unusual, even nonsensical, meaning.

What can you say about this text? Does it have any practical value?

2.1.3 vocabulary

The aim of these exercises is to show the importance of vocabulary in a work of fiction.

2.1.3.1 Write a text, using informal vocabulary.

2.1.3.2 Rewrite this text, using formal vocabulary, making changes when necessary.

2.1.3.3 Rewrite the text from 2.1.3.2, replacing some words with their synonyms, making changes when necessary.

Compare these three texts. What can you say about them?

2.2 object of description

2.2.1 Write a text which describes one or more objects, e.g., a table, a room, a picture, a landscape, etc.

2.2.2 Create a narrative based on the text in 2.2.1 by any technique you desire, such as the history of the object of description or how it was created, its analysis with the aim of determining its meaning, and so forth.

Smooth out the two texts if necessary, to make them read as a unit.

2.2.3 Write a text describing a chronologically or causally connected action, e.g., going out of a room into the street, a stroll down the street, a couple meeting and falling in love, etc.

2.2.4 Rewrite this text, adding greater details.

2.2.5 Shorten this text by removing some less important details.

Compare the three texts. What can you say about them?

2.3 tense

The aim of these exercises is to show the impact of tense in which action is described on a work of fiction.

2.3.1 Write a text in the present tense.

2.3.2 Rewrite the text from 2.3.1 in the past tense, making changes when necessary.

2.3.3 Rewrite the text from 2.3.1 in the future tense, making changes when necessary.

Compare these three texts. How do they differ? Which one seems the best? Why? If there are no essential differences between them, write a text where the differences are essential and one of the texts is the best.

2.4 manner of presentation

2.4.1 Rewrite the text from 2.1.1.1 or any other text in the form of a first person account of a character in the text.

Compare these two texts. How do they differ?

2.4.2 Write a text which consists exclusively of a dialogue.

2.4.3 Rewrite the text from 2.4.2, replacing the dialogue with the author's narration, making changes when necessary.

Compare these two texts. How do they differ?

2.4.4 Write a text consisting of a conversation between two or more people, including a description of how they behave, in the commonly accepted form, e.g., "Did you do it?" The woman asked sternly?/"Yes, I did," the man replied feebly, turning his eyes aside.

2.4.5 Rewrite the text from 2.4.4 in the script form, as in a play, augmenting it with stage directions if necessary, e.g., The Woman *(in a stern voice)*: Did you do it?/The Man *(feebly, turning his eyes aside):* Yes, I did.

2.4.6 Rewrite the text from 2.4.4, rendering the conversation as a narration using third person pronouns, changing it if necessary, e.g., Did he do it? Asked the woman in a stern voice./Yes he did, replied the man feebly, turning his eyes aside.

2.4.7 Rewrite the text from 2.4.4 as a straight narration, changing it if necessary, e.g., The woman asked the man in a stern voice if he had done it. He replied in a feeble voice that he did, turning his eyes aside.

Compare these four texts. How do they differ?

2.5 point of view

The aim of these exercises is to show the importance of the point of view on a work of fiction.

2.5.1 Write a text from the first person viewpoint ("I/we").

2.5.2 Rewrite the text from 2.5.1 from the third person viewpoint, using pronouns ("he/she/it/ they").

2.5.3 Rewrite the text from 2.5.1 from the third person viewpoint, using proper names ("John/Mary/Smith") without the use of pronouns.

2.5.4 Rewrite the text from 2.5.3, replacing the

proper names with the appropriate pronouns in places where you feel they are preferable.

2.5.5 Rewrite the text from 2.5.1, using the pronoun "you" in its universal sense.

Compare these five texts. How do they differ?

2.5.6 Write a new text from the third person viewpoint, using a pronoun or a proper name.

2.5.7 Rewrite the text from 2.5.6 from the first person viewpoint, using "I/we."

Compare these two texts. How do they differ? Are the differences in this case about the same as between the texts in 2.5.1 on the one hand and the texts in 2.5.2 and 2.5.4 on the other?

If there are no essential differences between the texts in 2.5.1 and 2.5.7 on the one hand and the derived respective third person texts on the other, try coming up with texts where this is true.

2.6 mode

2.6.1 Write a text with a sad story.

2.6.2 Rewrite the text from 2.6.1, making the story funny.

2.6.3 Rewrite the text from 2.6.1, making the story grotesque.

Compare these three texts. What can you say about them?

2.6.4 Write a text with a story, the end of which is unknown at the beginning.

2.6.5 Rewrite the text from 2.6.4, stating in the beginning how the story will end and modifying the text appropriately to make it effective if necessary.

Compare these two texts. Is either of them more effective than the other? What can you say about the two approaches?

2.6.6 Write a text with the action taking place in a dream.

2.6.7 Write a text with the action taking place in real life which corresponds to the situation in the text in 2.6.6 (that is, for which the text in 2.6.6 is a symbolic representation).

Compare these two texts. Which of them is more effective? What advantages does each of them have over the other?

2.6.8 Write a "nonsensical" text in a free-association way on the model of automatic writing.

Is the text completely nonsensical? Can you write a completely nonsensical text?

2.6.9 Rewrite the text from 2.6.8, making changes in it to make it "coherent."

Compare these two texts. What can you say about them?

2.6.10 Compose a text of an existing one by picking out sentences in it in random fashion.

Compare this text to that in 2.6.8. Is it nonsensical?

2.7 genre

Here the word "genre" refers to structurally different works.

2.7.1 Write a short text consisting of a self-contained story.

Give it more than one title and consider what impact each of them has on the story. Are they different? Which do you find the best? Why?

2.7.2 Write a text that constitutes a synopsis of an original work some 5-10 pages long.

2.7.3 Write a synopsis of an original novel.

How does it differ from the one in 2.7.2?

2.7.4 Write the first and last paragraph of this novel.

2.7.5 Write a synopsis of a film based on this novel.

2.7.6 Write a review of this film.

2.7.7 Write a text which constitutes the description of a fragment from this film which depicts one or more objects.

2.7.8 Write a text which constitutes the description of a fragment from this film which depicts action.

2.7.9 Rewrite the story of the novel in 2.7.3 in the form of a short letter to someone familiar.

Compare the texts in 2.7.3, 2.7.5, 2.7.6, and 2.7.9. What can you say about them? Was one of them easier to write than others? If so, then why?

2.7.10 Write an anecdote, making it as brief as possible.

2.7.11 Write a few concise epigrams.

Discuss them.

2.7.12 Write a scholarly or scientific article.

What can you say about the language in the text in 2.7.12 as compared to that in the texts in 1.3, 2.7.1, and 2.7.4?

2.8 structure

The aim of these exercises is to show different ways of structuring a work of fiction.

2.8.1 Write a synopsis of an original novel based on a plot (chronological development of a story). It should be a smoothly flowing narration. You can use the synopsis from 2.7.3 if the novel you wrote about falls into this category.

2.8.2 Write a synopsis of an original novel based on a principle other than chronology or plot, e.g., location, characters, type of action, period of time, etc. You can use the synopsis from 2.7.3 if the novel you wrote about there falls into this category. Unlike the text in 2.8.1, this will not constitute a smoothly flowing narration, but will be an enumeration of facts, features, events, actions, etc. There will have to be some criterion which will bind them into a whole, however.

2.8.3 Rewrite, or describe how you would rewrite, the text from 2.8.1, basing it on some nonchronological principle as defined in 2.8.2. What did you have to do to achieve this? What difficulties did you run into in your attempt?

2.8.4 Rewrite or describe how you would rewrite the text from 2.8.2, basing it on a plot. What did you have to do to achieve this? What difficulties did you run into in your attempt?

2.9 subject

The aim of these exercises is to improve the technique of developing subject and imagination.

2.9.1 Write a synopsis of a work based on a well-known subject— e.g., the Agamemnon cycle, the legend of Tristan and Isolde, the story of Raskolnikoff, etc.—replacing one or more essential elements of the original with new ones. In the Agamemnon cycle, for instance, the essential element is the unjust and insidious revenge of one person over another and its tragic consequences. In the legend of Tristan and Isolde, the essential element is the prohibition of illicit love and the latter's inevitable tragic end. In the Raskolnikoff story, the essential element is a horrific crime and the feeling of guilt it evokes which leads to a voluntary acceptance of punishment. Write a synopsis of the original work first and then that of your version.

2.9.2 Write a synopsis of the text in 2.9.1, replacing one or more essential elements of the original with different ones.

2.9.3 Write a synopsis of the text in 2.9.1, replacing one or more essential elements of the original with still different ones.

Compare these three texts. How do they differ?

2.9.4 Write a synopsis of a mininovel, as the term has been defined in literature (Yuriy Tarnawsky, "The Mininovel and Negative Text," *American Book Review*, May-June, 2007, reprinted in Yuriy Tarnawsky, *Claim to Oblivion*, JEF Books, 2016.), in other words a short work of fiction that relies on negative text (primarily omission of vital information), which is based on a well-known novel and which retains the intent and effect of the original. Limit your work to deleting information, without adding any vital information of your own. Write a synopsis of the original novel first and present your work in terms of it.

Discuss your work by comparing it with your own synopsis of the original novel.

2.9.5 Repeat the exercise of 2.9.4 for the same novel, changing to some degree the intent and effect of the original.

Discuss your work by comparing it with your own synopsis of the original novel.

2.9.6 Write a synopsis of an original mininovel, paying special attention to crafting the negative text.

Compare the three results. How do they differ?

3. drama

The aim of these exercises is to develop the technique of writing a play. They are based on the assumption that a play is a work of fiction with clearly delineated spatial and temporal limits (the space of the stage and the viewer's patience, respectively). It may include common prose texts (conversations, narrations) as well as poems.

The word "text" appearing in the exercises below has the same connotation as in the exercises dealing with prose, with the understanding that it is designed to be performed on the stage.

3.1 elements

This is what plays are made up of.

Although composed independently, the texts produced in these exercises should be conceived as parts of a unified work—a play some 2-5 pages long. The order of the composed scenes may be rearranged at the end to produce the final work.

3.1.1 spoken text

3.1.1.1 Write a text consisting exclusively of a dialog between two people.

3.1.1.2 Write a text consisting exclusively of a conversation between more than two people.

3.1.1.3 Write a text consisting exclusively of a narration by one person, describing an action.

3.1.1.4 Write a text consisting exclusively of a narration by one person, describing something other than action.

3.1.2 behavior

3.1.2.1 Fill out the text in 3.1.1.1 with a description of how the people behave as they talk.

3.1.2.2 Fill out the text in 3.1.1.2 with a description of how the people behave as they talk.

3.1.2.3 Fill out the text in 3.1.1.3 with a description of how the person behaves as he/she talks.

3.1.2.4 Fill out the text in 3.1.1.4 with a description of how the person behaves as he/she talks.

3.1.3 setting and character description

3.1.3.1 Write a text consisting of the description of the stage in the above texts.

3.1.3.2 Write a text consisting of the description of

the people in the above texts.

3.1.3.3 Put the texts produced in 3.1.2.1, 3.1.2.2, 3.1.2.3, 3.1.2.4, 3.1.3.1, and 3.1.3.2 together, making changes when necessary to produce a unified text, and give it a name.

3.2 manner

The aim of these exercises is to show the impact of the manner in which a story is told on the audience.

3.2.1 Assuming the behavior of the characters in the play developed in 3.1.3.3 was realistic, rewrite the latter, replacing the behavior of one or more characters in it with nonrealistic action which better conveys the nature of the situation, changing other elements if necessary. For instance, if a character was talking about something painful, he/she might be made carry a heavy object. Such action, in this context, might be labeled as metaphorical, related in a counterpoint fashion to the spoken words. If the person was described as crying, the action would be labeled as an illustration, relating to it as one part to another in musical harmony.

3.2.2 Rewrite the play developed in 3.1.3.3, changing as many of its elements as desired, without affecting the basic story to create a different but effective impact on the viewer.

Compare the three versions. What conclusions can you draw from the differences between them? Repeat these exercises a few times.

part two

exercises and sample texts

1. poetry

The aim of these exercises is to develop the technique of writing free verse. Here then, unless otherwise stated, the word "poem" is understand to mean a free verse poem.

1.1 nature of a poem

The aim of these exercises is to show the nature of the free verse technique—the freedom it gives the poet to express what drives him/her to write a poem.

1.1.1 Rewrite a well-known traditional poem, for instance one of Shakespeare's sonnets, in free verse, breaking it up into separate lines as your intuition tells you.

Comment: Using "Sonnet 18" by William Shakespeare.

Sonnet 18
Shall I compare thee to a summer's day?
Thou art more lovely and more temperate:
Rough winds do shake the darling buds of May,
And summer's lease hath all too short a date:
Sometime too hot the eye of heaven shines,
And often is his gold complexion dimm'd;
And every fair from fair sometime declines,
By chance or nature's changing course untrimm'd;
But thy eternal summer shall not fade

Nor lose possession of that fair thou ow'st;
Nor shall Death brag thou wander'st in his shade,
When in eternal lines to time thou grow'st:
So long as men can breathe or eyes can see,
So long lives this and, this gives life to thee.

Comment: Breaking up the original into lines and
changing punctuation.

Shall I compare thee
to a summer's day?
Thou art more lovely
and more temperate.
Rough winds do shake
the darling buds of May,
and summer's lease
hath all too short a date.
Sometime too hot
the eye of heaven shines,
and often
is his gold complexion
dimm'd,
and every fair
from fair
sometime declines
by chance
or natures changing course
untrimm'd.
But thy eternal summer
shall not fade,
nor loose possession
of that fair

thou ow'st,
nor shall Death brag
thou wonder'st in his shade,
when in eternal lines
to time thou grow'st.

So long as men can breathe
or eyes can see,
so long lives this,
and this gives life
to thee.

*1.1.2 Expand the poem from 1.1.1 by adding to it
your own associations, making changes in the
original without abandoning the original structure.*

Comment: Modifying the language while
expanding.

Should I compare you
to a summer day?
You are more beautiful
and more gentle.
Rough winds shake violently
spring's tender blossoms
and the lease that summer has secured
lasts way too short.
Sometimes the eye of heaven
stares too bright
and frequently its blinding gaze
grows dim.
And there are times when beauty

loses beauty
uglied by chance
or nature's fickle ways.

But your eternal summer
will not grow cold
and will not loose the beauty
it gets from you.
And death won't brag
you walk in its shade
as in immortal verses
you grow old.

As long
as there's a man
who breathes
and who can see
these lines will live
and you will live
in them.

*1.1.3 Trim the poem from 1.1.2 to its most
essential elements, strengthening it by the means
that free verse puts at your disposal.*

You
are more lovely
than a summer day.
With time
spring's tender blossoms
wither
and fall to the ground,

and the lease
that summer has secured
lasts way too short.
At times
the eye of heaven
stares too bright
and frequently
its blinding gaze
grows dim.
And there are times when beauty
loses beauty
uglied by chance
or nature's fickle ways.

But your eternal summer
will not grow cold
and will not lose the beauty
it gets from you.
And death won't brag
you walk in its shade
as in immortal verses
you grow old.

As long
as there's a man
who breathes
and who can see,
these lines will live
and you will live
in them.

1.1.4 Write your own poem on the same subject as

*the one in 1.1.1, departing from it as much as you
want and utilizing to the utmost the means the free
verse technique puts at your disposal.*

Sonnet 18

For K

Remember
that early June morning,
we stopped off
at the little half-abandoned palace
of some count or a famous writer,
turned into an agricultural school,
on the way to my home town
I hadn't seen for years?
We went walking
through the surrounding park,
this one really abandoned,
with huge trees
so tall you couldn't see their tops,
their canopies joining together
blocking out the sky,
birds singing in the leaves,
their voices echoing in the space below
as in a vast Gothic cathedral.
Someplace nearby
in the bushes
water in a fountain
or a brook
was making a sound
just like the birds above,

it was cool,
festive,
like an eternal holiday.
Being with you
is an eternal holiday.
It will end one day,
the same as you and I,
but the fact it existed,
was once,
will never die,
will live on forever,
even if there is no one to know it,
if these lines
are no longer there,
if there is no space or time
for them to be in.

*Compare these four poems. What can you say
about them?*

The 1.1.1 free verse variant imposes a particular
logical pattern on the poem, stressing some of its
elements and deemphasizing others. 1.1.2, in
addition to modernizing the language, clarifies
some of Shakespeare's intentions obscured by the
rigor of the sonnet form by expressing them in
more natural terms, for instance, "summer's lease
hath all too short a date > the lease that summer
has secured last way too short," "[eye] shines too
hot > stares too bright," [eye's] gold complexion >
blinding gaze," and "So long as men can breathe or
eyes can see > As long as there's a man who

breathes and who can see." Modernizing the language, unfortunately, gets rid of the delightful "darling buds of May" which were likely occasioned by the strictness of the sonnet form. Leaving them in seemed stylistically awkward. 1.1.3 deletes material which does not contribute to the author's intent, in particular the statement that "every fair from fair sometimes declines" which does not appear to have much relevance to the main tenet that beauty is eternal and summer is not. All three variants, however, remain marred by the iambic meter of the original which continues to shine through in places, making these free verse versions sound awkward. This is finally avoided in the variant in 1.1.4, which fully departs from the original, permitting the full power of the free verse technique to take effect and expressing a contemporary view of immortality.

Note that

> And every fair from fair sometime declines,
> By chance or nature's changing course
>   untrimm'd

may be interpreted as

> and there are times when beauty
> avoids other beauty
> because of chance
> or nature's crooked path.

Likewise,

> When in eternal lines to time thou grow'st:

could be interpreted as

> when you tread
> along the lines
> that lead to eternity.

Take another well-known classical poem and repeat the exercises.

Comment: Exercise skipped.

1.1.5 Rewrite a short prose text – e.g., a passage from a newspaper article, a physics textbook, a cookbook, etc.– in free verse, breaking it up into lines as your intuition tells you.

Comment: Using Stephen Hawking, *A Brief History of Time*, Bantam Books, 1996, p. 75.

The fourth category is the strong nuclear force which holds the quarks together in the proton and neutron, and holds the protons and neutrons together in the nucleus of an atom. It is believed that this force is carried by another spin-1 particle, called the gluon, which interacts only with itself and with the quarks. The strong nuclear force has the curious property called confinement: it always binds particles together into combinations which have no

color. One cannot have a single quark on its own
because it would have a color (red, green, or blue).

Comment: Breaking up the original into lines.

The fourth category
is the strong nuclear force
which holds the quarks together
in the proton and neutron,
and holds the protons and neutrons
together in the nucleus of an atom.
It is believed
that this force is carried
by another spin-1 particle,
called the gluon,
which interacts only with itself
and with the quarks.
The strong nuclear force
has the curious property
called confinement:
it always binds particles together
into combinations which have no color.
One cannot have a single quark
on its own
because it would have a color
(red, green, or blue).

1.1.6 Expand the poem from 1.1.5 with your own
associations as in 1.1.2.

The fourth
and final

category
is nature's strong and mighty
force
called nuclear
or central,
most essential,
which like an eagle's
steely talons
tightly holds
the quirky quarks
together
inside the nests of protons
and neutrons,
and also holds the two
together
as if one
in the tight nutshell
of the atom.
Some think
this force is carried
by another spin-1
particle,
called gluon,
which interacts with self
and the quarks.
This force
has the odd property
called confinement
which binds together
particles
into clusters
that have no color.

So
you can't have a quark
alone,
as it would have color,
would bloom
like a red, green, bright blue tulip,
rose.

*1.1.7 Shorten the poem from 1.1.6 to its most
essential elements.*

The fourth
and final
category
is nature's mighty
force
called nuclear
or central,
most essential,
which like an eagle's
steely talons
tightly holds
the quirky quarks
together
iinside the nests of protons
and neutrons,
and also holds the two
together
as if one
in the tight nutshell
of the atom.
Some think

this force is carried
by a particle,
called gluon,
which interacts with self
and the quarks.
This force
has the odd
property
which binds together
particles
into clusters
that have no color.

So
you can't have a quark
alone,
as it would have color,
would bloom
like a red, green, bright blue tulip,
rose.

Compare the original and these two poems.
Compare them to the four previous poems. What
can you say about them?

Breaking up the original text into lines in 1.1.5 was
of little value, as the new logical pattern of the
poem did not have much impact on its meaning.
The version in 1.1.6 is in a more effective pattern
adjusted to the new lexical matter which attempts
to turn the purely informative, scientific contents of
the text into poetry. In 1.1.7, very little pruning

was done, and even that was optional, most likely due to the scientific nature of the original text—much of what had to be done was already done in the previous attempt at "poeticizing" the text. In the text in 1.1.3 a lot of "detritus" had to be eliminated because of the poetic nature of the original text.

Take another prose text and repeat the exercises.

Comment: Exercise skipped.

1.2 structure of a poem

The aim of these poems is to show the importance of breaking up the text of a poem into lines.

1.2.1 Break up a well-known free verse poem into lines different from the original, adhering to the logic of the contents as your intuition tells you. (Here every line will constitute an autonomous meaningful unit.)

Comment: Using "Canto II" by Ezra Pound.

Canto II
(fragment)

Hang it all, Robert Browning,
There can be but the one "Sordello."
But Sordello, and my Sordello?

Lo Sordels si fo di Mantovana,
So-shu churned in the sea,
Seal sports in the spray-whited circles of cliff-wash,
Sleek head, daughter of Lir
          eyes of Picasso
Under black fur-hood, lithe daughter of Ocean;
and the wave runs in the beach-groove:
"Eleanor, Elenaus, and Eleptolis!"
          And poor old Homer blind, blind as a bat,
Ear, ear for the sea-surge, murmur of old men's
          voices:
"Let her go back to the ships,
Back among Grecian faces, lest evil come on our
          own,
Evil and further evil, and a curse cast on our
          children,
Moves, yes, she moves like a goddess
And has the face of a god
          and the voice of Schoeney's daughters,
And doom goes with her in walking,
Let her go back to the ships,
          back among Grecian voices."

Comment: Breaking up the original.

Hang it all,
Robert Browning,
there can be
but the one
"Sordello."
But Sordello,
and my Sordello?

Lo Sordels
si fo di Mantovana,
So-shu
churned in the sea,
seal sports
in the spray-whited
circles of cliff-wash,
sleek head,
daughter of Lir
eyes of Picasso
under black fur-hood,
lithe daughter of Ocean;
and the wave
runs in the beach-groove:
"Eleanor, Elenaus, and Eleptolis!"
And poor old Homer
blind,
blind as a bat,
ear,
ear for the sea-surge,
murmur
of old men's voices:
"Let her go back
to the ships,
back
among Grecian faces,
lest evil come on our own,
evil
and further evil,
and a curse
cast on our children,
moves, yes,

she moves
like a goddess
and has the face
of a god
and the voice
of Schoeney's daughters,
and doom goes
with her
in walking,
let her go back
to the ships,
back among
Grecian voices."

*1.2.2 Break up the poem from 1.2.1 into lines
which sometimes violate the logic of the contents.
(Here some lines will not constitute autonomous
meaningful units.)*

Hang it all, Robert
Browning, there can be
but the one "Sordello."
But Sordello, and my
Sordello? Lo Sordels
si fo di Mantovana,
So-shu churned in
the sea, seal sports
in the spray-whited
circles of cliff-wash,
sleek head, daughter
of Lir eyes of Picasso
under black fur-

hood, lithe daughter of
Ocean; and the wave
runs in the beach-
groove:
"Eleanor, Elenaus, and Eleptolis!"
And poor old Homer
blind, blind as a bat,
ear, ear for the sea-surge,
murmur of old men's
voices: "Let her go back
to the ships, back
among Grecian faces,
lest evil come on our
own, evil and further
evil, and a curse
cast on our children,
moves, yes, she
moves like a goddess and
has the face of a god
and the voice
of Schoeney's daughters, and
doom goes with her in
walking, let her go
back to the ships, back
among Grecian voices."

*1.2.3 Break up the poem from 1.2.2 further into
lines which violate the logic of the contents,
breaking up individual words where the effect is
interesting. (Here still more lines will not constitute
autonomous meaningful units.)*

Comment: Breaking up words and omitting punctuation.

Hang it
all Robert Brown
ing there can be but
the one "Sord
ello" but Sord
ello and my Sord
ello? lo Sord
els si fo di Man
tovana So-shu churn
ed in the sea sea
I sports in the spray
whited circles of cliff
wash sleek head
daughter of Lir eyes of
Picasso under black
fur hood lithe daughter
of Ocean and the wave
runs in the beach groove
Eleanor Elenaus, and Eleptolis
and poor old Homer
blind blind as a bat
ear ear for the sea surge murm
ur of old men's vo
ices Let her go back to
the ships back a
mong Grecian faces lest
evil come on our own evil
and further evil and
a curse cast on o

ur children move
s yes she move
s like a god
dess and has t
he face of a
god and the vo
ice of Schoeney's daughter
s and doom go
es with her in walk
ing let her go back
to the ships back a
mong Grecian vo
ices

1.2.4 Rewrite the poem from 1.2.1 as prose. Now it will constitute a single line.

Hang it all, Robert Browning, there can be but the one "Sordello." But Sordello, and my Sordello? Lo Sordels si fo di Mantovana, So-shu churned in the sea, seal sports in the spray-whited circles of cliff-wash, sleek head, daughter of Lir eyes of Picasso under black fur-hood, lithe daughter of Ocean; and the wave runs in the beach-groove: "Eleanor, Elenaus, and Eleptolis!" And poor old Homer blind, blind as a bat, ear, ear for the sea-surge, murmur of old men's voices: "Let her go back to the ships, back among Grecian faces, lest evil come on our own, evil and further evil, and a curse cast on our children, moves, yes, she moves like a goddess and has the face of a god and the voice of Schoeney's daughters, and doom goes with her in walking, let

her go back to the ships back among Grecian
voices."

*Compare these five poems. What can you say about
them?*

The broken up variation in 1.2.1 imposes a faster,
more dynamic rhythm on the poem, departing from
the slower, epic rhythm of the original. 1.2.2 jolts
the reader time and time again with the unexpected
breaks. He/she will be forced to pause but will
probably not have much difficulty to get the original
meaning. The overall effect, however, will be
significantly different from the original. 1.2.3 will
cause the reader to stop again and again, and
reread some of the lines a few times before
proceeding further, to get the correct
interpretation. New associations may then crop up
in his/her mind, making the poem blossom into
something different than the original poem. (This
may not be very pronounced in this example but
note to what effect this technique may be used
when composing an original poem with this effect in
the mind.) 1.2.4 leaves out any hint of a particular
rhythm of reading. In this case, because the
original consists of long ones, this version doesn't
differ much from the original. But imagine the
effect you would have if the original was composed
of short lines.

1.3 description

The aim of these exercises is to develop the technique of the treatment of poetic subject matter.

1.3.1 Write a poem dealing with a traditional "poetic" subject matter or object—for instance a rose, stars, autumn, etc.— referring openly to its features.

Rose 1

Incomprehensible rose,
Mona Lisa of flowers,
your fragrance—
a mysterious smile
on her blank face.

1.3.2 Write a poem on the same subject without using the words that openly describe it.

Rose 2

Blood sister
of willowy Renaissance ladies,
draped in fine silks,
how gracefully you don't move
in your still dance!

1.3.3 Write a poem on the same subject, using words which are in some way opposite to these words, for instance, meat, numbers, a geometric figure in the case of the examples mentioned above.

Rose 3

That shape, color
scent can co-
exist, have a
meaning, matter.

A theorem,
forever busy
proving itself.

Compare these three poems. What can you say about them?

The poem in 1.3.1 openly speaks of the rose's features, augmenting them with an allusion to Michelangelo's iconic painting. The one in 1.3.2 does this purely indirectly. It is only the title which tells us the subject of the poem is a rose. References to Mona Lisa and Renaissance ladies relate the two poems. The poem in 1.3.3 avoids mentioning anything about the rose's appearance and turns the text into a philosophical statement about the nature of things—does anything in life have meaning and value? The poem suggests that the rose's beauty may be a justification for its existence. It can be viewed as an antithesis to the thesis proposed in the first two poems.

*1.3.4 Write a poem in the first person singular ("I")
about the person.*

I 1

My heart
pounding loudly
in my chest,
I open the door
and there,
standing before me,
I see myself,
barely holding in my arms
something
that looks like
either my own
limp body
or a sheaf
of wilted lilies.

I 2

My heart
pounding loudly
in my chest,
I open the door
and there,
standing before me,
I see myself,
barely holding in my arms
something
that looks like

either my own
limp body
or a huge
bundle of weeds.

*1.3.5 Rewrite the poem from 1.3.4 in the third
person singular ("he/she"), modifying it as needed.
If no modification other than pronoun substitution is
needed, rewrite the poem from1.3.4 so that such
changes would be needed.*

He 1

His heart
pounding loudly
in his chest,
he opens the door
and there,
standing before him,
he sees himself,
barely holding in his arms
something
that looks like
either his own
limp body
or a sheaf
of wilted lilies

He 2

His heart
pounding loudly

in his chest,
he opens the door
and there,
standing before him,
he sees himself,
barely holding in his arms
something
that looks like
either his own
limp body
or a huge
bundle of weeds.

*Compare these two poems. What can you say
about them?*

All four poems deal with the same subject—a man
coming face to face with himself and concluding he
is in bad shape. "I 1," however, sounds
sentimental, since the author shows too much self-
pity—in effect says, "I am like a bundle of wilted
lilies." "I 2," avoids this, as here the author
compares himself to a bundle of weeds. In addition
to avoiding sentimentality, this is a poetically more
powerful statement because the author stresses his
own degradation by comparing himself to a plant
that is generally considered worthless. " I 1,"
therefore should be deemed inferior to "I 2."

In 1.3.5 the situation is different. Both poems
appear to be acceptable. In "He 1," it is someone
else who speaks about the person and here self-pity

does not come into play. In fact, for some readers, this poem may better convey the author's compassion for the person as it compares him to a plant which is a symbol of innocence.

1.3.6 Write a poem describing an object, for instance an apple.

Apple 1

Pale green
world of empty
rooms, tall clear
windows, hardwood
floors, the sound of bare
children's feet, voices,
laughter
echoing above them.

1.3.7 Write a poem describing the same object as it sees itself.

Apple 2

Tart white
space
stretching
in all directions
to a thin
pale green
horizon.

The law four
over three pi
r cubed rules the
world.

*Compare these two poems. What can you say
about them?*

The poem in 1.3.6 represents the view of a person
contemplating a pale green apple. The images
reflect the person's impressions from having
consumed a similar apple before and apples in
general. The references to clearness and emptiness
are suggested by the whiteness of the inside of an
apple and perhaps the effect of its delicate tart
taste. The reference to children could be a memory
from childhood associated with apples. The poem
in 1.3.7 attempts to render such an apple's concept
of itself. The volume of a sphere with radius r is
$4/3\ \pi\ r^3$.

*1.3.8 Write a poem dealing with an event (action)
in the present tense.*

Comment: Using "I 2" from 1.3.4.

I Present

My heart
pounding loudly
in my chest,
I open the door

and there,
standing before me,
I see myself,
barely holding in my arms
something
that looks like
either my own
limp body
or a huge
bundle of weeds.

1.3.9 Write a poem dealing with the same event in the past tense, making changes when necessary.

I Past

My heart
pounding loudly
in my chest,
I opened the door
and there,
standing before me,
I saw myself,
barely holding in my arms
something
that looked like
either my own
limp body
or a huge
bundle of weeds.

1.3.10 Write a poem dealing with the same event in

the future tense, making changes when necessary.

I Future

A day will come
when,
my heart
pounding loudly
in my chest,
I'll open the door
and there,
standing before me,
I'll see myself,
barely holding in my arms
something
that'll look like
either my own
limp body
or a huge
bundle of weeds.

*Compare these three poems. What can you say
about them?*

All three poems appear acceptable. The past tense
version didn't require any changes other than those
of tense. In the case of the future tense version,
although the present tense form could have been
used, it was felt that changing is beginning
improved the poem. This version also seems at
least a bit more effective than the other two,
perhaps because the poem is written in the first

person mode and it seems more painful for one to anticipate one's decline than to state that it is occurring or has already occurred.

1.4 poetic image

The aim of these exercises is to develop the technique of creating poetic image and stimulating imagination.

1.4.1 Create an unusual simile, for instance, "Water like a hump on a person's back."

Mirror like a hump on a person's back.
Mirror like a soft pillow.
Mirror like a pit in the ground.

1.4.2 Create a construction with an epithet corresponding to the simile in 1.4.1, for instance, "Hunchbacked water."

Hunchbacked mirror.
Soft mirror.
Excavated mirror.

1.4.3 Create a metaphor in the form "noun phrase 1 of noun phrase 2" that corresponds to the simile in 1.4.1, for instance, "The hump of water."

The hump of the mirror.
The pillow of the mirror.

The pit of the mirror.

1.4.4 What images do these constructions evoke in your mind? For instance, "Water looking like a hunchbacked person. The hunchback of water.

Deformed water. A hunchbacked sea. The hump of the sea. Water on crutches. The sea on crutches." and so forth.

The world sticking out of the mirror like a hump on a person's back. A hunchbacked world. The hunchback of the world in the mirror. The Quasimodo of the world hiding behind objects in the mirror.

Burying your face in the mirror. Clutching a mirror in your sleep. Oh, sweet mirror! Dreaming in a mirror. Clear mirror dreams.

An excavated world. The world gone in the bottomless pit of the mirror. The world in the mirror like a roomful of broken furniture piled up in a pit. Facing yourself in the black pit of the mirror. Your excavated face. Your excavated life.

1.4.5 What opposite images do these constructions evoke in your mind? For instance, "Slender water. A slender sea. Water looking like a princess. The young prince of the sea." and so forth.

The world in the mirror like a slender young man.

The prince of mirrors. The world in the mirror like a Renaissance portrait of a handsome young man. The Renaissance courtyards of mirrors. The Renaissance world of mirrors.

Washing your face in the mirror. Splashing the cold water of the mirror over your face first thing in the morning. Laughing out loud on seeing yourself in the mirror as if from a splash of cold water.

Fresh morning air streaming into the room through the mirror. A mirror like a window open wide into an apple orchard. Climbing into the apple orchard world of the mirror.

Permute the order of the above exercises and go through the specified steps. Repeat the exercise a few times.

Comment: Exercise skipped.

1.4.6 Create an image based on a compound noun construction, e.g., "A cloud is a skybruise." List associated images the image evokes, e.g., "A bruised sky. The sky beaten black and blue. The sky has been in a bad fight."

A cloud is a dreamstone. Huge soft rocks of clouds in the sky. Clouds are dreams of stones. Clouds are what rocks dream to be. Clouds have the shapes of dreams. A cloudy sky is a dream quarry. The sky has a moonache. The moon like a huge white tooth. Moonlight like a bad toothache. The moon aching like a huge white tooth. The night sky twisted out of shape by moonlight like a face by a toothache.

A watch is a timebrook. The purling of time inside a watch. A mountain brook flowing through a watch. A brook is a liquid watch. The ticking of water. Water in a brook like the mechanism inside a Swiss watch.

1.4.7 Describe in a few words an object or a phenomenon, then create a poetic image of it as it pops into your head and proceed improving the image until you feel it has reached its full potential, e.g., "A red comet in the night sky. A comet blazing through the night sky, its red tail trailing behind it. A comet blazing through the night sky, its red hair streaming   behind it. A mad comet speeding through the night sky, its long red hair streaming behind it. A mad comet speeding naked   through the night sky, its long red hair streaming behind it."

A hot muggy day in the woods. The stifling air of summer woods. The sweaty air of summer woods. The green armpits of summer woods. The sweaty armpits of summer woods. The smelly armpits of summer woods.

White clouds on the horizon. Huge piles of white laundry spilling over the horizon. Huge piles of celestial laundry spilling over the horizon. Huge piles of wet celestial laundry spilling over the horizon. Huge mounds of celestial laundry ready to be ironed piled up on the horizon.

Pink clouds in the evening sky. Pink and white clouds in the evening sky. Pink and white Rubensian clouds in the evening sky. Pink and white Rubensian ladies in the evening sky. Pink and white Rubensian ladies lolling around in the evening sky.

1.4.8 Create a compact poetic image (metaphor, simile, etc.) and expand it into a description with the original image at its core, e.g., "Fists of clouds. Clouds rioting above the city, their angry fists raised high."

Shriveled stars. It'd been a hot dry summer and the stars were appropriately meager like apples on a long neglected apple tree that'd grown wild. They hung forlornly, small and shriveled, in the puny night sky.

Oboes of apples. All through the night he heard through his sleep the sound of apples hitting the ground in the orchard streaming in through the open window like oboes playing long low soft notes.

Apple planets. Out in the garden apples were orbiting a huge apple tree like so many shiny red planets moving helter-skelter past each other.

1.4.9 Create a few original puns.

What is a camelemac?—A palindromedary.

What do you call a cat that hasn't turned out the way it was supposed to?—A catastrophe.

And what about a cat that is terrific?—Magnificat.

He is Ruthless—his wife Ruth has left him.

He's no longer a racist—he has stopped racing and now just jogs.

Her periods are so light, they should be called commas.

How do they compare to metaphors and other tropes?

At the heart of all tropes lies some kind of semantic clash—a difference between the normal meaning of the word or phrase and the meaning in the particular situation—which has to be resolved in order for the utterance in which they occur to be properly interpreted. In the metaphoric statement "The dog of wind howls outside my window," for instance, the word "dog" has lost its meaning of being an animal with a head, trunk, tail, and four legs, having the ability to bark, etc., and has retained only that of being capable of emitting the sounds of howling, which are transferred to the physical phenomenon of rapid movement of air. This is because a rapid movement of air is incapable of possessing the aforementioned attributes of a canine but is capable of making a sustained loud sound. In other words, the phrase merely states that the wind outside the window sounds like a howling dog. Similarly, in the metonymic statement "Fifty head of cattle ran through the gate," the word "head" has lost all of the attributes of a head except that of being able to be counted, since heads cannot run through gates on their own. (One way of counting cattle is by pointing to their heads.)

In a pun, a word with one meaning is placed into a spot which another word, denoting something else but sounding like it, is supposed to occupy, as happens with the word "period" in the last example above, which can mean "menstruation" and "punctuation mark." The situation in puns differs from those in tropes in that no semantic adjustment of the type just described is necessary for their proper interpretation, but similar in that they also involve a clash between the meanings of two words.

2. prose

The aim of these exercises is to develop the technique of writing fiction (but see 2.7.12 below).

The tasks spelled out in the exercises below connected with texts, unless otherwise noted, refer to narrations, that is, should constitute descriptions of objects or actions and be roughly between 100 and 500 words long.

2.1 language

The aim of these exercises is to show the influence of language on a work of fiction.

2.1.1 syntax

These exercises concentrate on the field of syntax. They show the influence of syntax on a work of fiction.

2.1.1.1 Write a text in what you consider to be your "normal" language.

On coming home from work, John washed up, made his supper, and sat down to eat. It was after five in the afternoon but, it being summer, the sun was still high up and the giant boulder of its light was squashing down the urban landscape below. Its effect was well pronounced on the flat roofs of the buildings seen through the fourth-floor window but appeared to be nonexistent on the tall smokestack of the asphalt plant about a mile away where John worked. It stood erect and firm, emitting a blue smudge of smoke into the smoggy sky like the memory of a thread.

2.1.1.2 Rewrite the text from 2.1.1.1, eliminating compound sentences and making changes when necessary.

On coming home from work John washed up. He then made his supper. After that he sat down to eat. It was after five in the afternoon. It being summer, the sun was still high up, however. The giant boulder of its light was squashing down the urban landscape below. Its effect was well pronounced on the flat roofs of the buildings seen through the fourth-floor window. It appeared to be nonexistent on the tall smokestack of the asphalt plant about a mile away where John worked, however. It stood erect and firm, emitting a blue smudge of smoke into the smoggy sky like the memory of a thread.

2.1.1.3 Rewrite the text from 2.1.1.2, eliminating subordinate clauses and making changes when necessary.

On coming home from work John washed up. He then made his supper. After that he sat down to eat. It was after five in the afternoon. It being summer, the sun was still high up, however. The giant boulder of its light was squashing down the urban landscape below. Its effect was well pronounced on the flat roofs of the buildings seen through the fourth-floor window. It appeared to be nonexistent on the tall smokestack of the asphalt plant about a mile away, however. This is where John worked. The smoke stack stood erect and firm, emitting a blue smudge of smoke into the smoggy sky like the memory of a thread.

2.1.1.4 Rewrite the text from 2.1.1.3, replacing noun modifiers and similar constructions with simple sentences, wherever possible, making changes when necessary.

John came home from work. He washed up. He made his supper. He then sat down to eat. It was after five in the afternoon. It was in the summer. As a consequence, the sun was still high up. Its light seemed a boulder. The boulder seemed huge. It seemed to be squashing down the urban landscape below. This was especially true of the roofs of the buildings. They were all flat. You could see this through the fourth-floor window. There was a smokestack visible in the distance. It rose up into the sky. It was tall. It was about a mile away. It was part of an asphalt plant. This is where John worked. Unlike the buildings, the smokestack seemed unaffected by the sunlight. It stood erect. It stood firm. It emitted a smudge of

smoke into the smoggy sky. The smoke was blue.
It seemed the memory of a thread.

*2.1.1.5 Rewrite the text from 2.1.1.4, introducing
into it compound sentences, subordinate clauses,
and conjunctions only where this is necessary, to
make it more natural.*

John came home from work. He washed up. He
made his supper. He then sat down to eat. It was
in the summer. It was after five in the afternoon.
As a consequence, the sun was still high up. Its
light seemed a boulder. The boulder seemed huge.
It seemed to be squashing down the urban
landscape below. This was especially true of the
roofs of the buildings. They were all flat. You could
see this through the fourth-floor window. There was
a tall smoke stack visible rising up into the sky
about a mile away. It was part of an asphalt plant
where John worked. Unlike the buildings, the
smokestack seemed unaffected by the sunlight. It
stood erect and firm. It emitted a smudge of blue
smoke into the smoggy sky. It seemed the
memory of a thread.

*Compare these five texts. What is the difference
between them? What general conclusions would
you draw from the texts? What distinguishes the
text in 2.1.1.4 from that in 2.1.1.5?*

In the original text in 2.1.1.1 the reader's attention
is focused on what is considered to be the most

important facts and events in the story—that John washed up, cooked his supper, sat down to eat, that it was five in the afternoon, and so forth. Other facts and events, such as that prior to the former events he had been at work, that those events took place a home, that it was summer, and so forth, are assigned a secondary role. This semantic hierarchy of the information is accomplished through the hypotactic nature of the text, the composition of its sentences, and their main and subordinate clauses. With each successive simplification of the syntactic structure of the sentences, as the text becomes gradually more and more paratactic, this meaning hierarchy is lost progressively more and more, culminating in the text in 2.1.1.4 in which essentially all facts and events are assigned equal importance. The text in 2.1.1.5 pulls back somewhat from that position, relegating some of the information to secondary level. So, whereas the text in 2.1.1.4 is highly segmented and artificial-sounding, that in 2.1.1.5 is somewhat less so and seems more natural.

Another aspect of what is happening in the rewriting of the above texts is that they acquire a progressively more and more pronounced pattern, culminating in that of 2.1.1.4. The text in 2.1.1.5 once more recedes somewhat from that position. This pattern is primarily syntactic—in particular the consistent NP VP, optional NP, structure of the sentences—but also lexical, such as the repetition of pronouns and the emergence of anaphora.

Nevertheless, the reader without doubt will become aware of it the same as he/she would become aware of the rhythm in a text written in regular meter. Once he/she learns the pattern, then, he/she will anticipate its reoccurrence as, for instance, in a text written in hexameter.

One may conclude that texts endowed with this type of pattern have the same advantages and disadvantages as those written in regular meter, that is, that they may appear repetitive and therefore boring for some readers, and pleasing, because their development may be anticipated, for other. It is up to the writer to decide whether structuring his/her text in this manner is suitable to his/her goal.

Comment: For more on the subject of the impact of syntax on a literary work see "The Effect of Grammar Restrictions on a Literary Work" in Yuriy Tarnawsky, *Claim to Oblivion*, JEF Books, 2016.

2.1.1.6 Rewrite the text from 2.1.1.1 as one sentence, making changes when necessary.

On coming home from work after five in the afternoon John washed up, made his supper, and sat down to eat, but, it being summer, the sun was still high up and the giant boulder of its light was squashing down the urban landscape below, its effect being well pronounced on the flat roofs of the buildings seen through the fourth-floor window, appearing to be nonexistent, however, on the tall smokestack of the asphalt plant about a mile away where John worked, standing erect and firm, emitting a blue smudge of smoke into the smoggy sky like the memory of a thread.

Compare these six texts. What distinguishes the text in 2.1.1.6 from the preceding ones?

The text in 2.1.1.6, because of the continuous stream of its only partly structurally marked language, loses some of the hypotactic quality of the text in 2.1.1.1 without creating a new paratactic structure. The distinction between the main and subordinate clauses is obscured by the uninterrupted flow of words, causing facts and events become fused into what may seem for some to be a single complex semantic unit. Texts of this type are sometimes confused with stream of consciousness texts although they do not belong to this category.

2.1.1.7 Write what you consider to be a stream of consciousness text, that is, a text that is defined as internal monologue that describes the process going on in a mind in which external information is intermixed with internally engendered thoughts.

No laurel bushes here to be trimmed. Just garbage. Piles of it. With the light reflected off them like from waxy leaves. Laurel leaves. Not to be trimmed. It's hot. The street's empty too.

Everyone's dropped dead like flies in a closed up room. Except me. Dragging my feet along the sidewalk. Scraping it. Scraping them. Wearing out the heels. Barely able to move. After eight hours in that stinking joint. Day after day. For how many years now? Fourteen? Seventeen? Can't even remember. What's the difference three years more or less.   Speaking of a stinking joint. Should I drop in at Stinkin' Joe's to have a pint? Naaah. I stinks too much. Of piss and beer. Enough of that other stink. Tar. And smoke. Too tired too. And hungry. Got to get home and fix my supper. And wash up first. Get that smell of tar smoke off my skin and out of my hair. And of sweat from my armpits. Would add it to the stink of beer and piss if I'd visit Stinkin' Joe's. Too many stinks. Look at that smokestack. Straight and thin like from another landscape. Where they trim laurel bushes. Beautiful. And that smoke coming out of it's beautiful too. Real thin. And blue. Like the memory of a thread. Blue thread.

What can you say about the text in 2.1.1.7? How does it compare with the text in 2.1.1.6?

Syntactically, the text in 2.1.1.7 consists mostly of language fragments rather than well-formed sentences, as one frequently encounters in conversations. It is paratactic but also highly fragmented. The understand it, the reader must fill in the missing language matter which makes it meaningful. Semantically, as the definition of stream of consciousness states, it is a monologue taking place in the narrator's mind. The text in 2.1.1.6, by contrast, is a narration by an external observer in which the sentence markers (periods, etc.) have been replaced by commas, making it hard for the reader to determine whether the sentences are independent or parts of another sentence.

Comment: What is the reason for laurel bushes and their trimming being here? Try to find out on your own if you care to know.

2.1.2 punctuation

The aim of these exercises is to show the influence of punctuation on a work of fiction.

2.1.2.1 Rewrite the text from 2.1.1.6 without punctuation marks, making changes when necessary to make it better understandable.

On coming home from work after five in the afternoon John washed up made his supper and sat down to eat but it being summer the sun was still high up and the giant boulder of its light was squashing down the urban landscape below its effect being well pronounced on the flat roofs of the buildings seen through the fourth-floor window but appearing to be nonexistent on the tall smokestack of the asphalt plant about a mile away where John worked the former standing erect and firm emitting a blue smudge of smoke into the smoggy sky like the memory of a thread.

How does the text in 2.1.2.1 compare with the text in 2.1.1.6?

Because of a total lack of structural markings, the text in 2.1.2.1 takes on even more of the qualities of the text in 2.1.1.6 described above. Furthermore, potential ambiguities introduced by a lack of structural marking in texts of this type make the likelihood of semantic fusion in them still greater. This still doesn't make the text a stream of consciousness text, as can be seen by comparing it to the text in 2.1.1.7.

2.1.2.2 Rewrite the text from 2.1.2.1 with punctuation marks, inserting them at times in different places from those in the text in 2.1.1.1, in order to change its effect or meaning. If the text in 2.1.2.1 is not amenable to this, write another text and do the exercise with it.

On coming home from work, after five in the afternoon, John washed up. Made his supper. And sat down. To eat. But, it being summer, the sun was still high. Up. And the giant boulder of its light was squashing down the urban landscape. Below. Its effect being well pronounced on the flat roofs. Of the buildings. Seen through the fourth-floor window. But appearing to be nonexistent on the

tall smokestack. Of the asphalt plant. About a mile
away. Where John worked. The former standing
erect. And firm. Emitting a blue smudge. Of
smoke. Into the smoggy sky. Like the memory.
Of a thread.

*What can you say about this text? Does it have any
practical value?*

Because of having been broken up into language
fragments, the text has taken on the structural
characteristics of a stream of consciousness text,
while remaining a narration by an external
observer. The reader may be puzzled by this but in
the end may construe that it is in fact an internal
monologue by someone constructing a narration of
a series of events. This particular text isn't very
effective but texts of this type crafted carefully may
be of value in exercises dealing with reshaping of
meaningful texts.

*2.1.2.3 Rewrite the text from 2.1.2.1 with
punctuation marks, inserting them at times in
different places from those in the text in 2.1.1.1, in
order to give it an unusual, even nonsensical,
meaning.*

On coming home. From work after five. In the
afternoon John washed up. Made his supper and
sat down to eat but it. Being summer, the sun was
still high up and the giant. Boulder of its light was
squashing down the urban landscape. Below its

effect being well pronounced on the flat. Roofs of the buildings seen through the fourth-floor window but appearing to be nonexistent. On the tall smokestack of the asphalt. Plant about a mile away where John worked the former standing. Erect and firm emitting a blue smudge. Of smoke into the smoggy. Sky like the memory of a thread.

What can you say about this text? Does it have any practical value?

This text is even harder to interpret that the text in 2.1.2.2 and for some may appear to be nonsensical. (See the exercises 2.6.8-2.6.10 for more on the topic of nonsensicalness.) Still, texts of this type, crafted with care, may be of value in exercises dealing with reshaping of meaningful texts.

2.1.3 vocabulary

The aim of these exercises is to show the importance of vocabulary in a work of fiction.

2.1.3.1 Write a text, using informal vocabulary.

So frigging hot in here! And stuffy. But it's a heck of a lot better than outside. It's like being roasted alive out there. Had to stop off at that watering hole across from the church on the way home. A real dive! Stunk of piss and beer. Had a couple of pints. Suds really cool you down. Except now it's worse. Dripping like a pig. I mean leaking like a rusty slop pail.

2.1.3.2 Rewrite this text, using formal vocabulary, making changes when necessary.

It is extremely hot in here. It is also close. But it is much better than outside. It is like being in an oven out there. I had to visit that bar across from the church on the way home. What a run-down place! It smelled of urine and beer. I had a couple of glasses. Beer really cools one down. Except now I feel worse. I am sweating like a pig. I mean, I am leaking like a rusty bucket.

2.1.3.3 Rewrite the text from 2.1.3.2, replacing some words with their synonyms, making changes when necessary.

It's devilishly hot in here. And stuffy. But it's a lot better than outside. It's like a furnace out there. I had to drop into that bar across from the church on the way home. What a dirty joint! It reeked of urine and beer. I had a couple of mugs. Beer really cools you down. Except now I feel worse. I'm sweating like a swine. I mean, I'm leaking like a bucket full of holes.

Compare these three texts. What can you say about them?

In this particular case the original text in 2.1.3.1 appears to be the best, probably because of its nature—a first person account of a raunchy situation, well-suited for informal speech. Both of the two derived texts are acceptable, with the one from 2.1.3.2 perhaps a bit better than that from 2.1.3.3 because it is stylistically more consistent. In the text in 2.1.3.3 you have a mixture of somewhat formal and less formal words.

2.2 object of description

2.2.1 Write a text which describes one or more objects, e.g., a table, a room, a picture, a landscape, etc.

Comment: Photograph described:

Loyalist Militiaman at the Moment of Death, Cerro Muriano [Spain], September 5, 1936, by Robert Capa.

This is Robert Capa's best-known photograph, purportedly describing a Spanish loyalist militiaman being shot during the early days of the Spanish Civil War. We were unable to get permission to use it in the text, but it is readily available on the internet by searching on the title.

This is a grainy black and white photograph of rather poor quality, roughly twice as wide as high.

It shows a man falling backwards on the background of what appears to be a clear sky and a gently sloping hill covered with short and sparse, seared grass that looks like spilled gasoline burning. The sky takes up about the top two thirds of the picture. The slope descends left to right, revealing gradually more and more of a hilly rural landscape devoid of buildings, trees, and people, with a low mountain range in the distance.

The man takes up the two lower thirds of the left half of the photograph. He is middle aged, thin, almost haggard, European-looking but with a dark complexion. He wears what looks like a black military cap on his head with a high peak up front and is dressed in a white shirt with rolled up sleeves, light, civilian-style pants, and shoes which are only partly visible in the picture. Over his right shoulder he carries something resembling a small canvas pouch hanging on a thin strap or rope and has two wide black leather straps going down over his chest with two cartridge pouches on the bottom held together by a belt. The man's eyes and mouth are closed and his head turned left, so that only the right side of his face is showing. His feet are way up in front, as if having slipped out from under him, his knees bent, and he is falling down backwards, turning slightly to the left, and will ultimately land on his seat. His right arm is stretched straight out to the right and the rifle he has been holding is flying out of his hand. It is of the bolt type, has a strap attached to it for carrying, and is still partly

clutched by the man's thumb and apparently index
and middle fingers, but will soon be let go
completely. His left arm is not visible. The sunlight
is strong, bleaching everything white and the man
casts a sharp shadow on the ground, black and
narrow, like the trunk of a gnarled tree.

*2.2.2 Create a narrative based on the text in 2.2.1
by any technique you desire, such as the history of
the object of description or how it was created, its
analysis with the aim of determining its meaning,
and so forth.*

The photograph appears to show a soldier falling in
battle after being shot. He is obviously not a
regular soldier, however, but a militiaman. So the
photograph most likely comes from a civil war.
Given the appearance of the landscape and that of
the man, this would probably have been in the
south of Europe, most likely again in one of the
Mediterranean countries. The clothing the man
wears and the look of the rifle date the picture at
some time in the 1930's or 40's. It would appear,
therefore, that the photograph comes from the
Spanish or Greek Civil War, with the first being the
more likely choice because of the appearance of the
man, the rifle, and the landscape. The Greek
insurgents frequently wore military clothing and
carried more modern-looking weapons, and the
topography of Greece is generally more rugged
than that in the picture. Moreover, the Spanish
Civil War aroused much more interest among the

journalists and the public than the Greek one, and
it is, therefore, more likely that a photograph from
it would have been publicized.

But is the picture what it appears to be? The aim of
the photograph must have been to represent a
soldier falling in battle rather than one whose feet
have slipped out from under him. Who would
bother photographing and publicizing such a trivial
event? But had the man been shot in reality, it
would have happened from the front, as he was
charging down the hill. He couldn't have been shot
from the back while running away because of being
shielded by the crest behind him. It is also unlikely
he was shot from the left because why would he
have been running past people shooting at him?
There is no possibility of his being shot from the
right. But being shot from up front, while charging,
he most likely would be falling forward. This would
be so because of the inclination of the terrain and
his own momentum. The rifle then also would have
been flying forward rather than to the side. And
the way the man is falling very strongly suggests he
is imitating what he thinks would have happened
had he been shot. As was said, his left arm is not
visible. Its shadow is also not visible on the ground.
He must be sticking it out downward so as to break
his fall which is unlikely if he were shot. And
another reason why it is unlikely that the man was
shot from the front is the angle from which the
picture was taken. The man is being photographed
from the left and up front. The photographer, then,

would have been lying or sitting on the ground (given the angle of the shot he couldn't have been standing up) with his back turned to the enemy and thus would have been an even better target than the charging soldier.

One may also claim that the man has not been shot at all because there is no sign of his being hit anywhere on his body. But this would not be a good argument. A bullet hitting a person probably wouldn't be visible in a photograph. Yet this would not be true, however, of an explosion, a large shell, or a number of bullets, such as those from an automatic weapon, all of which would have left visible signs. So, we may only conclude that the man was not hit in such a way and also that, if he had been hit, he wasn't killed instantly but merely wounded, even if perhaps mortally.

It is therefore to be assumed that the picture was staged. The photographer chose a spot for himself and asked the man to run down the hill with the rifle in his hand and then fall suddenly as if having been hit. He may even have given the man some instructions, such as, for instance, "Throw your rifle away and fall back in a dramatic way." Or the man may have done it spontaneously, imagining this is the way one falls after being shot. The pose may in some way even have been suggested to the man by the image of crucified Christ—eyes and mouth closed, head tipped to one side, and arms spread wide. (But here the man can't stop himself from instinctively sticking his left arm out to break his fall.) This would be supported by the likelihood that the photograph is from Spain rather than from Greece. The presence of crucifixes in Spain is much more widespread than in Greece, where the Byzantine tradition dominates. This would be true even of a militiaman, such as the man in the photograph, a person in all likelihood anticlerical and perhaps even an atheist. His outlook would still have been strongly shaped by the Catholic Church.

But, in spite of all these arguments, we cannot completely discount the possibility that the picture shows a soldier falling in battle after being shot, that it doesn't come from Spain, and that it is not from the 1930's. Photographs can be as ambiguous as ink blots.

Smooth out the two texts if necessary, to make them read as a unit.

Comment: The two texts already form a unit and do not require any changes.

2.2.3 Write a text describing a chronologically or causally connected action, e.g., going out of a room into the street, a stroll down the street, a couple meeting and falling in love, etc.

He steps out onto the landing and proceeds down the stairs. Murky light from the skylight laced with the acrid smell of cat urine fills the cramped space. The stairs turn left all the time like an idiot child playing its dull, incomprehensible game. Spokes in the railing are like a meaningless sound emitted in accompaniment. The landing at the bottom is pitch-black and he has to grope his way to the door and unlatch it in order to step outside. The fresh air is like a shout of joy. Free at last! The street runs steeply up to the right, but it is a challenge he will willingly take on. (111 words)

2.2.4 Rewrite this text, adding greater details.

He steps out onto the landing, shuts the door, turns around, gets his keys out of his pocket, locks it, puts the keys back in, turns left, and proceeds down the two flights of stairs. Brown murky light from the skylight high above laced with the acrid smell of cat urine fills the cramped narrow space. The stairs turn left, and left, and left, like an idiot child playing its dull, incomprehensible game. Spokes in the railing, repeated over and over, are like a short meaningless sound emitted in accompaniment, huh, huh, huh, huh, huh.... The landing at the bottom is pitch-black and he has to grope his way to the door, find the latch, and pull on it in order to step outside. The fresh clear air is like a shout of joy. Free at last! He shuts the door behind him and turns right. The street runs steeply up, almost as if to spite him, but it is a challenge he will willingly take on. (167 words)

2.2.5 Shorten this text by removing some less important details.

He steps out onto the landing, shuts the door, and proceeds down the stairs. Brown murky light from the skylight high above laced with the acrid smell of cat urine fills the cramped narrow space. The stairs turn left, and left, and left, like an idiot child playing its dull, incomprehensible game. Spokes in the railing, repeated over and over, are like a short meaningless sound emitted in accompaniment, huh, huh, huh, huh, huh…. The landing at the bottom is pitch-black and he has to grope his way to the door and unlatch it in order to step outside. The fresh clear air is like a shout of joy. Free at last! He shuts the door and turns right. The street runs steeply up, almost as if to spite him, but it is a challenge he will willingly take on. (140 words)

Compare the three texts. What can you say about them?

All of the texts are acceptable, but each creates a different effect. The first text is terse, concentrating on the essential actions of the character, leaving up to the reader to fill in the details. He/she may skip these to hurry along with the character to see what happens next. The second text overwhelms the reader with minute details, seemingly slowing down the action and bringing in an element of drudgery into the narration. The third text is a compromise between the two and probably close to what one normally encounters in a "mainstream" narration. It is up to the author to decide which effect he/she wants to evoke in the reader.

2.3 tense

The aim of these exercises is to show the impact of tense in which action is described on a work of fiction.

2.3.1 Write a text in the present tense.

Comment: Using text in 2.2.3 for "Text 1."

Text 1

He steps out onto the landing and proceeds down the stairs. Murky light from the skylight laced with the acrid smell of cat urine fills the cramped space. The stairs turn left all the time like an idiot child playing its dull, incomprehensible game. Spokes in the railing are like a meaningless sound emitted in accompaniment. The landing at the bottom is pitch-black and he has to grope his way to the door and unlatch it in order to step outside. The fresh air is like a shout of joy. Free at last! The street runs steeply up to the right, but it is a challenge he will willingly take on.

Text 2

I cross the footbridge over the narrow stream,
unsteady like its memory in my mind, descend the
three steps leading into the street, cross it, and
walk up the path toward the cluster of buildings like
clouds gathered at the top of the hill. My
grandmother, parents, siblings, I myself of those
years long gone are not there, but I feel them like
the sound of their voices spoken seconds earlier,
ringing in my ears. I pass the main house, round its
corner, and walk into the dense orchard, dark like
the shadow cast by the huge house. There I lie
down in the tall grass, shut my eyes, and release
life from my body like breath I have held for too
long.

*2.3.2 Rewrite the text from 2.3.1 in the past tense,
making changes when necessary.*

Text 1

He stepped out onto the landing and proceeded
down the stairs. Murky light from the skylight laced
with the acrid smell of cat urine filled the cramped
space. The stairs turned left all the time like an
idiot child playing its dull, incomprehensible game.
Spokes in the railing were like a meaningless sound
emitted in accompaniment. The landing at the
bottom was pitch-black and he had to grope his
way to the door and unlatch it in order to step
outside. The fresh air was like a shout of joy. Free

at last! The street ran steeply up to the right, but it was a challenge he would willingly to take on.

Text 2

I crossed the footbridge over the narrow stream, unsteady like its memory in my mind, descended the three steps leading into the street, crossed it, and walked up the path toward the cluster of buildings like clouds gathered at the top of the hill. My grandmother, parents, siblings, I myself of those years long gone were not there, but I felt them like the sound of their voices spoken seconds earlier, ringing in my ears. I passed the main house, rounded its corner, and walked into the dense orchard, dark like the shadow cast by the huge house. I lay down there in the tall grass, shut my eyes, and released life from my body like breath I had held for too long.

2.3.3 Rewrite the text from 2.3.1 in the future tense, making changes when necessary.

Text 1

He will step out onto the landing and proceed down the stairs. Murky light from the skylight laced with the acrid smell of cat urine will fill the cramped space. The stairs will turn left all the time like an idiot child playing its dull, incomprehensible game. Spokes in the railing will be like a meaningless sound emitted in accompaniment. The landing at the bottom will be pitch-black and he will have to grope his way to the door and unlatch it in order to step outside. The fresh air will be like a shout of joy. Free at last! The street will run steeply up to the right, but it will be a challenge he will willingly take on.

Text 2

I will cross the footbridge over the narrow stream, unsteady like its memory in my mind, descend the three steps leading into the street, cross it, and walk up the path toward the cluster of buildings like clouds gathered at the top of the hill. My grandmother, parents, siblings, I myself of those years long gone will not be there, but I will feel them like the sound of their voices spoken seconds earlier, ringing in my ears. I will pass the main house, round its corner, and walk into the dense orchard, dark like the shadow cast by the huge house. There I will lie down in the tall grass, shut my eyes, and release life from my body like breath I have held for too long.

Compare these three texts. How do they differ? Which one seems the best? Why? If there are no essential differences between them, write a text where the differences are essential and one of the texts is the best.

The three versions of "Text 1" all sound roughly the same, with none of them appreciably better than the other two. With "Text 2," the present and past tense versions seem inferior, perhaps even inappropriate, especially the first one, given the topic of a person returning to his/her past with the aim of expiring there. The future tense version is the only one that is fully acceptable, given the nonrealistic nature of the final statement, making it a possibility rather than a fact. Note that if the text had been a third person account ("he/she" instead of "I"), all three texts would have been acceptable, but with the third one still perhaps a shade better.

2.4 manner of presentation

2.4.1 Rewrite the text from 2.1.1.1 or any other text in the form of a first person account of a character in the text.

Comment: Using the text from 2.1.1.1.

It was after five in the afternoon when I got home from work but, it being summer, the sun was still high up. It was real hot too. I live on the fourth floor and it looked like the whole city was being squashed down by the sunlight as by a gigantic boulder—some sort of a transparent meteorite or something. This was especially true of the buildings with flat roofs, which are way in the majority. The only thing that wasn't affected was the smokestack in the plant where I work—the asphalt plant—which is about a mile away. It rose way up into the sky, a smudge of smoke streaming out of it, merging with the smoke already in the air, so that you could barely see it. As I always do, I first washed up, and then fixed my supper, and sat down to eat.

Compare these two texts. How do they differ?

The first-person account, of necessity, is less formal and carries more emotional information. It is also less linear, jumping back and forth between various subtopics.

2.4.2 Write a text which consists exclusively of a dialogue.

So, what did you do yesterday after work?

It was so damned hot I had to stop off at Stinkin' Joe's on the way home and have some beer.

Did you stay there long?

Naaah,... just had a pint. It stinks too much of piss there and besides I was too tired. Was practically falling off the stool. Went home, washed up, and had supper.

Where do you wash? In the kitchen sink? You said you don't have a bathroom.

No, I do have a bathroom. But it's just a toilet. I usually wash up in the kitchen sink but it was full of dishes, so I used the washbasin I have for that purpose. Filled it with water and washed in it. I put it on a stool by the kitchen window so I can look outside as I wash. It's nice. Makes you feel classy.

2.4.3 Rewrite the text from 2.4.2, replacing the dialogue with the author's narration, making changes when necessary.

It was a scorching hot summer day and on his way home from work at the asphalt plant John stopped off at Drinking Joe's Bar, popularly known as Stinkin' Joe's because of its unsanitary nature, to cool off with a beer. He had only one drink, however, because he felt tired and the smell of urine which has permanently permeated the place bothered him too much. After finishing his drink, he dragged himself to his apartment which is about a mile away, washed up, fixed his supper, and sat down to eat. His bathroom has only a toilet and he uses the kitchen sink for washing up, but the latter was full of dirty dishes, so John washed up in the washbasin he keeps for such purposes, which, as he always does, he put on a stool by the kitchen window, so as to be able to look outside. He likes to do this as it makes him feel as if he lived in a classier place.

Compare these two texts. How do they differ?

The narration text provides greater details. It

would have been harder to provide them in a dialogue. The dialogue text, on the other hand, carries more emotional information.

2.4.4 Write a text consisting of a conversation between two or more people, including a description of how they behave, in the commonly accepted form, e.g., "Did you do it?" The woman asked sternly?/"Yes, I did," the man replied feebly, turning his eyes aside.

"Did you do it?" The woman asked sternly.

"Yes, I did," the man replied feebly, turning his eyes aside. He looked uncomfortable in his body as if in tight-fitting clothes.

"You're not very convincing," the woman said. "Am I supposed to believe you?"

"Believe me or not, I don't care," the man said. "But I did it. Except not in the way you wanted me to."

2.4.5 Rewrite the text from 2.4.4 in the script form, as in a play, augmenting it with stage directions if necessary, e.g., The Woman (in a stern voice): Did you do it?/The Man (feebly, turning his eyes aside): Yes, I did.

The woman *(in a stern voice):* Did you do it?

The man *(in a feeble voice, turning his eyes aside):* Yes, I did. *(He looked uncomfortable in his body as in tight-fitting clothes.)*

The woman *(pressing on):* You're not very convincing. Am I supposed to believe you?
The man *(this time firmly, visibly annoyed):* Believe me or not, I don't care. But I did it. Except not in the way you wanted me to.

2.4.6 Rewrite the text from 2.4.4, rendering the conversation as a narration using third person pronouns, changing it if necessary, e.g., Did he do it? Asked the woman in a stern voice./Yes he did, replied the man feebly, turning his eyes aside.

Did he do it? The woman asked sternly.

Yes, he did, the man replied feebly, turning his eyes aside. He looked uncomfortable in his body as if in tight-fitting clothes.

He's not very convincing, the woman said, pressing on. Was she supposed to believe him?

Believe him or not, he didn't care, the man said this time firmly, visibly annoyed. But he'd done it. Except not in the way she wanted him to.

2.4.7 Rewrite the text from 2.4.4 as a straight narration, changing it if necessary, e.g., The woman asked the man in a stern voice if he had done it. He replied in a feeble voice that he did, turning his eyes aside.

The woman asked the man in a stern voice if he had done it.

He replied feebly that he did, turning his eyes aside. He looked uncomfortable in his body as if in tight-fitting clothes.

Pressing on, the woman said that he wasn't very convincing and asked if he expected her to believe him.

Speaking this time firmly, visibly annoyed, the man said that he didn't care if she believed him or not, but that he had done it, except not in the way she wanted him to.

Compare these four texts. How do they differ?

Written in the standard dialogue form, the text in 2.4.4 may be viewed as neutral. It is best suited for a work conceived as "normal" or "mainstream."

The script text in 2.4.5 puts the reader in a "play," mode, perhaps making him/her visualize the scene more graphically. Note that the parenthetical sentence in the man's first answer is given in the past tense, the same as in the text in 2.4.4, since it is assumed the text is part of a work of fiction. If it were part of a play, it would have been rendered in the present tense, as it would refer to an actor standing on the stage. If the text is part of a work of fiction, it may impact the perception of the entire work, making it appear nonstandard. A potential benefit of this form is elimination of the usually vacuous refrain of "X asked/Y replied," "she said/he said," etc. that typically occurs in the normal form. Bear in mind that the "he" and "she" in 2.4.6, although they could have antecedents outside the dialog, refer to the man and woman in it. Being even more unusual than the text in 2.4.5, this text is at least as likely to color the reader's perception of the entire work as nonstandard as the one in 2.4.5.

The text in 2.4.7 shows the common way of rendering dialog in narration form and is again best suited for works conceived as "normal" or "mainstream."

2.5 point of view

The aim of these exercises is to show the importance of the point of view on a work of fiction.

2.5.1 Write a text from the first person viewpoint ("I/we").

My name is John. I live in a big industrial city in the first half of the twentieth century, in a cold water, one bedroom, kitchen, and bathroom fourth-floor apartment. The bathroom has only a toilet in it and I have to wash up in the kitchen sink or a washbasin which I have to fill up. I live alone and work in an asphalt plant which is about a mile away. My job is dirty and I have to wash up well when I come home before making my supper. I really stink when I come home. I use strong, good quality laundry soap because it does the job better, which I buy in big square chunks cut with a knife that look like bricks. This is especially true because the soap is dark yellow, almost brown, looking really like glazed brick. I lather myself well in the armpits to wash out the smell of sweat, and then wash off thoroughly with water. The fact the water is cold doesn't bother me. I like washing up in the washbasin because I can put it on top of a tall stool I have by the kitchen window and enjoy the view outside as I wash. It makes me feel like I live in a classier joint than I actually do, with a big bathroom with a window in it. I take my time drying myself off with a towel while staring out the window. It is this part of the washing I like the best. From the window I can see the flat roofs of the buildings stretching as far as the eye can see all the way to the horizon, which prevail in the city, and smokestacks rising here and there above them into the sky. The biggest one is the one in the asphalt plant where I work but there are many more all over the town which look progressively smaller and smaller as they get farther away until you can barely see the ones on the horizon. I like seeing smoke coming out of the smokestacks, especially when it's windy, which makes it look like hair blowing in the wind. It is as if the smokestacks were strange-looking people, tall and thin, without arms and faces, with long wispy hair that the wind is messing around with. I like thinking such thoughts.

2.5.2 Rewrite the text from 2.5.1 from the third person viewpoint, using pronouns ("he/she/it/ they")

His name is John. He lives in a big industrial city in the first half of the twentieth century, in a cold water, one bedroom, kitchen, and bathroom fourth-floor apartment. The bathroom has only a toilet in it and he has to wash up in the kitchen sink or a washbasin which he has to fill up. He lives alone and works in an asphalt plant which is about a mile away. His job is dirty and he has to wash up well when he comes home before making his supper. He smells strongly of sweat when he comes home. He uses strong, good quality laundry soap because it does the job better, which he buys in big square chunks cut with a knife that look like bricks. This is especially true because the soap is dark yellow, almost brown, looking really like glazed brick. He lathers himself well in the armpits to wash out the smell of sweat, and then washes off thoroughly with water. The fact the water is cold doesn't bother him. He likes washing up in the washbasin because he can put it on top of a tall stool he has by the kitchen window and enjoys the view outside as he washes. It makes him feel like he lives in a nicer place than he actually does, with a big bathroom with a window in it. He takes his time drying himself off with a towel while staring out the window. It is this part of the washing he likes the best. From the window he can see the flat roofs of the buildings stretching as far as the eye can see all the way to the horizon, which prevail in the city, and smokestacks rising here and there above them into the sky. The biggest one is the one in the asphalt plant where he works but there are many more all over the town which look progressively smaller and smaller as they get farther away until you can barely see the ones on the horizon. He likes seeing smoke coming out of the smokestacks, especially when it's windy, which makes it look like hair blowing in the wind. It is as if the smokestacks were strange-looking people, tall and thin, without arms and faces, with long wispy hair that the wind is messing around with. He likes thinking such thoughts.

2.5.3 Rewrite the text from 2.5.1 from the third person viewpoint, using proper names ("John/Mary/Smith") without the use of pronouns.

The man's name is John. John lives in a big industrial city in the first half of the twentieth century, in a cold water, one bedroom, kitchen, and bathroom fourth-floor apartment. The bathroom has only a toilet in it and John has to wash up in the kitchen sink or a washbasin which John has to fill up. John lives alone and works in an asphalt plant which is about a mile away. John's job is dirty and John has to wash up well when John comes home before making his supper. John smells strongly of sweat when John comes home. John uses strong, good quality laundry soap because it does the job better, which John buys in big square chunks cut with a knife that look like bricks. This is especially true because the soap is dark yellow, almost brown, looking really like glazed brick. John lathers John well in the armpits to wash out the smell of sweat, and then washes off thoroughly with water. The fact the water is cold doesn't bother John. John likes washing up in the washbasin because John can put it on top of a tall stool John has by the kitchen window and enjoys the view outside as John washes. It makes John feel like John lives in a nicer place than John actually does, with a big bathroom with a window in it. John takes his time drying John off with a towel while staring out the window. It is this part of the washing John likes the best. From the window John can see the flat roofs of the buildings stretching as far as the eye can see all the way to the horizon, which prevail in the city, and smokestacks rising here and there above them into the sky. The biggest one is the one in the asphalt plant where John works but there are many more all over the town which look progressively smaller and smaller as they get farther away until you can barely see the ones on the horizon. John likes seeing smoke coming out of the smokestacks, especially when it's windy, which makes it look like hair blowing in the wind. It is as if the smokestacks were strange-looking people, tall and thin, without arms and faces, with long wispy hair that the wind is messing around with. John likes thinking such thoughts.

2.5.4 Rewrite the text from 2.5.3, replacing the proper names with the appropriate pronouns in places where you feel they are preferable.

The man's name is John. John lives in a big industrial city in the first half of the twentieth century, in a cold water, one bedroom, kitchen, and bathroom fourth-floor apartment. The bathroom has only a toilet in it and John has to wash up in the kitchen sink or a washbasin which he has to fill up. John lives alone and works in an asphalt plant which is about a mile away. John's job is dirty and he has to wash up well when he comes home before making his supper. John smells strongly of sweat when he comes home. John uses strong, good quality laundry soap because it does the job better, which he buys in big square chunks cut with a knife that look like bricks. This is especially true because the soap is dark yellow, almost brown, looking really like glazed brick. John lathers himself well in the armpits to wash out the smell of sweat, and then washes off thoroughly with water. The fact the water is cold doesn't bother him. John likes washing up in the washbasin because he can put it on top of a tall stool he has by the kitchen window and enjoys the view outside as he washes. It makes him feel like he lives in a nicer place than he actually does, with a big bathroom with a window in it. John takes his time drying himself off with a towel while staring out the window. It is this part of the washing he likes the best. From the window John can see the flat roofs of the buildings stretching as far as the eye can see all the way to the horizon, which prevail in the city, and smokestacks rising here and there above them into the sky. The biggest one is the one in the asphalt plant where John works but there are many more all over the town which look progressively smaller and smaller as they get farther away until you can barely see the ones on the horizon. John likes seeing smoke coming out of the smokestacks, especially when it's windy, which makes it look like hair blowing in the wind. It is as if the smokestacks were strange-looking people, tall and thin, without arms and faces, with long wispy hair that the wind is messing around with. John likes thinking such thoughts.

2.5.5 Rewrite the text from 2.5.1, using the pronoun "you" in its universal sense.

Your name is John. You live in a big industrial city in the first half of the twentieth century, in a cold water, one bedroom, kitchen, and bathroom fourth-floor apartment. The bathroom has only a toilet in it and you have to wash up in the kitchen sink or a washbasin which you have to fill up. You live alone and work in an asphalt plant which is about a mile

away. Your job is dirty and you have to wash up
well when you come home before making your
supper. You really stink when you come home. You
use strong, good quality laundry soap because it
does the job better, which you buy in big square
chunks cut with a knife that look like bricks. This is
especially true because the soap is dark yellow,
almost brown, looking really like glazed brick. You
lather yourself well in the armpits to wash out the
smell of sweat, and then wash off thoroughly with
water. The fact the water is cold doesn't bother
you. You like washing up in the washbasin because
you can put it on top of a tall stool you have by the
kitchen window and enjoy the view outside as you
wash. It makes you feel like you live in a nicer
place than you actually do, with a big bathroom
with a window in it. You take your time drying
yourself off with a towel while staring out the
window. It is this part of the washing you like the
best. From the window you can see the flat roofs of
the buildings stretching as far as the eye can see all
the way to the horizon, which prevail in the city,
and smokestacks rising here and there above them
into the sky. The biggest one is the one in the
asphalt plant where you work but there are many
more all over the town which look progressively
smaller and smaller as they get farther away until
you can barely see the ones on the horizon. You
like seeing smoke coming out of the smokestacks,
especially when it's windy, which makes it look like
hair blowing in the wind. It is as if the smokestacks
were strange-looking people, tall and thin, without

arms and faces, with long wispy hair that the wind is messing around with. You like thinking such thoughts.

Compare these five texts. How do they differ?

Of the five versions of the text, the one in 2.5.1 and 2.5.4 sound the most natural, the first one perhaps a bit more, since it was conceived with the first person viewpoint in mind. The text in 2.5.2, although acceptable, sounds somewhat strange, since there seems to be no justification for the use of "he" in this situation instead of a proper name. There should be something in the nature of the story which would call for it—perhaps something universal, so that "he" could refer to a generic male character. The fact that the man's name is introduced at the beginning of the text makes this impossible. A similar objection can be made to the text in 2.5.5, with the universal "you," which openly points at the reader. This version would very likely sound better with a more universal story. The text in 2.5.3 is the least acceptable because of a proper name being used throughout it, contrary to the common rules of rhetoric and in places perhaps even grammar. The text in 2.5.4 corrects theses transgressions.

Note that some changes had to be introduced into the derived texts to make them sound better — rephrasing the first sentence in the text in 2.5.3, and replacing the emotionally colored expressions "really stink" by "strongly smells" in the texts in 2.5.2, 2.5.3, and 2.5.4, and "classier joint" by "nicer place" in the texts in 2.5.2 , 2.5.3, 2.5.4, and 2.5.5. The use of such vocabulary in texts of this type is unusual.

In spite of the strangeness of the texts in 2.5.2, 2.5.3 and 2.5.5, it shouldn't be assumed that the approaches used in them should never be employed. There may be situations where their strangeness may be used to good effect. Note the feeling of alienation evoked by the text in 2.5.3. It shouldn't be too hard to think of a story where this would be desirable, for instance an autopsy report. Writing requires creativity on all levels, and breaking a rule of means being creative.

2.5.6 Write a new text from the third person viewpoint, using a pronoun or a proper name.

There is a man who lives in apartment 401 on the fourth floor of the building at 400 Concrete Street. He lives by himself and works at the Municipal Asphalt Plant which is a mile away. He is in his mid-forties, tall and thin, with a narrow bony face and dark blond hair which he wears short. His face is always clean-shaven. He keeps to himself and hasn't been seen talking to anyone since moving into his place five years ago. It has been rumored he is mute.

2.5.7 Rewrite the text from 2.5.5 from the first

person viewpoint, using "I/we."

I live in apartment 401 on the fourth floor of the building at 400 Concrete Street. I live by myself and work at the Municipal Asphalt Plant which is a mile away. I am forty-four years old, tall and thin, and have a narrow bony face and dark blond hair which I wear short. I am always clean shaven. I keep strictly to myself and I haven't talked to anyone since moving into my place five years ago. I suspect some people think I am mute.

Compare these two texts. How do they differ? Are the differences in this case about the same as between the texts from 2.5.1 on the one hand and the texts from 2.5.2 and 2.5.4 on the other?

In spite of a number of changes having been introduced into the first person viewpoint text in 2.5.7 to make it read smoothly, it may still sound awkward to some readers. People don't normally speak this way of themselves. The original third person viewpoint text in 2.5.6 is clearly more natural. Comparison of these two texts and of those of the preceding four seems to suggest that it isn't only the linguistic material in a text that is conditioned by the point of view, but also the information in it. Different things are apparently talked about depending on what viewpoint a text is conceived in. But it shouldn't be excluded that there are situations in which this sort of strangeness, as was the case with the text in 2.5.3, may be exploited to good purpose.

If there are no essential differences between the texts in 2.5.1 and 2.5.7 on the one hand and the derived respective third person texts on the other, try coming up with texts where this is true.

Comment: The differences seem essential.

2.6 mode

2.6.1 Write a text with a sad story.

His Father's Death 1

They notified John that his father was in a critical state in a hospital and that he should come as soon as possible if he wanted to see him alive. The two of them had had a serious falling out when John was still young and had not been in contact for years, but the prospect that his father was dying washed away all the anger and resentment he still harbored toward him in his heart and he hurried as fast as he could to the latter's bedside. John lived in another city and it was a half-day's trip for him to come, but he made it to the hospital before noon the next day, taking a taxi from the train station to make sure he would get there in time. In normal circumstances he relied on public transportation. They told him at the front desk what floor he should go to, and after inquiring at the nurses' station when he got there, he was shown to the room his father lay in and, with his heart pounding in his chest, he crossed its threshold and slowly walked toward the bed. The room was half dark and John could barely make out the still, shrunken form practically indistinguishable from the bed sheets stretched out in the high hospital bed before him, so unlike the vigorous man in the prime of his life he saw last. His heart sank. Did he come too late? Was his father dead? His eyes were closed and hands crossed on his stomach. Softly, like a thief, he walked up to the bed and placed his hands on those of his father's. They didn't respond to his touch but felt warm.

"Hi, dad, it's me, John," he said barely audibly, giving his father's hands a gentle squeeze, and remained standing in this position, hoping with all his might for an answer. None came, however, and as the hands under his continued being lifeless, John began to suspect that he was witnessing the last moments of his father's life. It looked like he indeed had come too late.

2.6.2 Rewrite the text from 2.6.1, making the story funny.

His Father's Death 2

They notified John that his father was in a critical state in a hospital and that he should come as soon as possible if he wanted to see him alive. The two

of them had had a serious falling out when John
was still young and had not been in contact for
years, but the prospect that his father was dying
washed away all the anger and resentment he still
harbored toward him in his heart and he hurried as
fast as he could to the latter's bedside. John lived
in another city and it was a half-day's trip for him
to come, but he made it to the hospital before noon
the next day, taking a taxi from the train station to
make sure he would got there in time. In normal
circumstances he relied on public transportation.
They told him at the front desk what floor he should
go to, and after inquiring at the nurses' station
when he got there, he was shown to the room his
father lay in and, with his heart pounding in his
chest, he crossed its threshold and slowly walked
toward the bed. It was dark in the room but John
could make out the shape of his father lying
stretched out under the covers in the high hospital
bed. He was unrecognizable. Years and the
disease had absolved themselves well of their task.
When John saw him last, his father was a vigorous
man in the prime of his life, with thick black hair, a
chiseled masculine face like those of virile
statesmen they put in the profile pose on coins, and
a wiry athletic body. What lay before him now
looked more like an open grave covered with a
sheet from one end of which stuck out what looked
like the head of an Egyptian mummy, with a shiny
bald skull, sunken cheeks, and a sharp, curving
nose. The only sign that he was alive was his eyes
which turned toward John as he was nearing the

bed.

"Hi, dad, it's me, John," John said softly, with tears welling up in his eyes. "I hope you don't mind I've come."

"Hi, Don," his father replied in a pale stain of a voice, turning his eyes to him and barely moving his head. "How are you today?"

Did he say "John" or "Don?" John wondered, and at first settled for the former, thinking he misheard what his father had said, but then concluded it was actually the latter, which he explained by his father's condition—illness and age. It was possible, he further mused, his father had forgotten what his name was, since they hadn't communicated for so long.

"Did you see the lawyer?" His father rasped again after a few seconds. "Did you talk to him?"

"What lawyer?" John asked, surprised.

"The one I told you about yesterday," his father replied. "About the will. You are to be the executor."

"I didn't see you yesterday, dad," John said emphatically. "I haven't seen you for years. I've come to apologize for that and to tell you I've missed you all that time and that I love you."

"I love you too, Don," his father whispered. "That's why I'm leaving all of my estate to you. You've been a wonderful son to me. Not like the others."

John was speechless. Was his father being sarcastic and was berating him in this snide way for not having been in contact with him for so long? This would be true to his nature. He'd always been an impossible person to get along with and it looked like he'd remained the same even on his death bed. He turned red with embarrassment and a thought started to form itself in his mind that he'd made a mistake in coming. It would have been better if he'd stayed at home.

Just at that instant he heard noises behind his back and as he turned around, he saw the nurse who had ushered him to his father's room accompanied by a tall husky man entering the room.

"I'm sorry, Mr. Johnson," she said as they both came up to him. "You're in the wrong room... with the wrong Mr. Johnson. This is *this* Mr. Johnson's father. Your father's room is a few doors down. It's my fault. Excuse me."

"Oh, yes, yes... I'm sorry," John stuttered, beginning to understand what had happened, and seeing the man before him, embarrassed, extended his hand toward him and, as the man took it in his, said, "Don?" and then, "John," when the latter replied with a loud, "Yes."

"Pleased to meet you," John said, shaking the man's hand and, turning red in the face, added, "I'm sorry," let go of the man's hand, and walked out of the room. The nurse followed closely behind him.

"How is my father, by the way?" He asked after regaining his composure, as they were walking side by side down the corridor.

"Amazing," she replied. "He's gotten much better during the night.... Pinched my bottom this morning."

Oh, God, John thought, it looks like he's his usual self and it's going to be difficult. I probably shouldn't have come.

2.6.3 Rewrite the text from 2.6.1, making the story grotesque.

His Father's Death 3

They notified John that his father was in a critical state in a hospital and that he should come as soon as possible if he wanted to see him alive. The two of them had had a serious falling out when John was still young and had not been in contact for years, but the prospect that his father was dying washed away all the anger and resentment he still harbored toward him in his heart and he hurried as fast as he could to the latter's bedside. John lived

in another city and it was a half-day's trip for him
to come, but he made it to the hospital before noon
the next day, taking a taxi from the train station to
make sure he would got there in time. In normal
circumstances he relied on public transportation.
They told him at the front desk what floor he should
go to, and after inquiring at the nurses' station
when he got there, he was shown to the room his
father lay in and, with his heart pounding in his
chest, he crossed its threshold and slowly walked
toward the bed. It was dark in the room but John
could make out the shape of his father lying
stretched out under the covers in the high hospital
bed. He was unrecognizable. Years and the
disease had absolved themselves well of their task.
When John saw him last, his father was a vigorous
man in the prime of his life, with thick black hair, a
chiseled masculine face like those of virile
statesmen they put in the profile pose on coins, and
a wiry athletic body. What lay before him now
looked more like an open grave covered with a
sheet from one end of which stuck out what looked
like the head of an Egyptian mummy, with a shiny
bald skull, sunken cheeks, and a sharp, curving
nose. His hands were crossed on his stomach and
eyes wide open, staring at the ceiling.

"Hi, dad, it's me John," John said softly on coming
up to the bed, not wanting to startle his father.

The latter didn't respond in any way, continuing to
stubbornly bore with his gaze into the ceiling. He

seemed in great pain—John noticed that his eyes were open much wider than one would have expected, practically bulging out of their sockets, and his breathing was rapid and shallow.

Moved, John put his hands on those of his father and gave them a gentle squeeze.
Then something happened he totally didn't expect—his father's hands grabbed his and squeezed them so hard, he nearly yelled out in pain.

Holding himself back, trying to speak as softly as possible, John said, "Dad, dad," but his father squeezed his hands ever harder with no sign of planning to stop.

John tried to free himself from the grip by twisting his hands and pulling back with them, but his father's body suddenly stiffened and rose up under the sheet, as if trying to form a bridge, and then, with an incredible force, the latter pulled on him and made him fall face down on top of himself. John felt as if he were falling into a grave. A vague thought passed through his mind that what was probably happening was that his father was going through his death throes.

In pain and terror, forgetting his concern, John yelled at the top of his voice, "Stop, dad, stop!" and, "No, no!" trying to free himself and to stand up but his father wouldn't let him go. It felt as if the two of them were joined into one forever.

Then unexpectedly again, a bunch of strong hands grabbed him by the shoulders from behind, lifted him up, and, with a little more effort, freed him from his father's grip.

Greatly relieved, John turned around and saw three figures—a tall husky man and two nurses standing before him. It was they who had come to his help.

"What in God's name are you doing, man?!" the man yelled angrily, pushed him aside and leaned over his father, obviously with the aim of comforting him.

Angered and offended, John was about to start explaining what had happened, but one of the nurses grabbed him by the arm and pulled him out of the room. The other one joined the man attending to his father.

"My father...." John started explaining himself, but the nurse didn't let him continue as she led him down the corridor.

"He's not your father, Mr. Johnson," she said. "I'm sorry. He's the other Mr. Johnson's father."

"What do you mean?" John mumbled, not understanding, his thoughts unable to arrange themselves into cohesion.

"We took you to the wrong room," the nurse said.

"It's our fault. We thought you were the other gentleman... son of *that* Mr. Johnson. Please forgive us. Your father's room was the one before it."

"Then why aren't we going there?" John asked with surprise, stopping abruptly, realizing they were going in the opposite direction.

"He's no longer there. I'm awfully sorry," the nurse replied. "He died during the night. I'm taking you to the morgue."

Compare these three texts. What can you say about them?

All three texts seem equally effective in telling their story. In this particular case they are look like independent texts, each describing a different tale. They do illustrate, however, that a story may be adapted to a different mode of presentation and that, in composing a work, the author has many choices as to how to address the reader.

2.6.4 Write a text with a story, the end of which is unknown at the beginning.

A Homecoming 1

As always, it was 5:30 sharp when John stepped out of the train on his way home from the office and the hands of the clock high up on the station tower dutifully pointed each to its proper spot on

the dial, dead still, as if welded there for good. This
was the only position he ever saw them in, being
too rushed to check the clock in the morning. His
house was less than a mile away and even if he
walked at a leisurely stroll pace, as always again,
he would be there by quarter to six.

The day was beautiful and warm for early May, and
after walking for a few minutes John took off his
jacket and carried it draped over his left arm to
better enjoy the weather, while holding his
briefcase in his right hand. He enjoyed feeling the
balmy air on his skin as it pushed its way in through
the fabric of his shirt. The sky was pale blue and
clear, and only here and there little while clouds
would scurry across it one after the other, jumping
up and down and from side to side like railroad cars
in an old suburban train carrying their passengers
home after a day's work in the city. The cars
nowadays were big and heavy and they charged
thundering ahead, only the resting places of their
final destination on their mind.

John thought of the strong little arms of his son and
daughter which would wrap themselves around his
neck as he would squat down to welcome them
when he stepped into the driveway, of the smooth
perfumed cheek of his wife which she would offer
him for a kiss when he stepped into the kitchen,
and the tasty supper he would be consuming in a
matter of minutes, with all four of them seated at
the dining room table, which she prepared to

welcome him home with. Another couple of hundred feet and his house sprung into view—pale blue on the background of the dark green trees around it, as if an emissary of the sky above them. The grass of the immaculate lawn he toiled over each Saturday looked like a giant green wedge driven deep into the ground and the shadow of the huge sycamore tree next to the house resembled a giant black ball restring on the ground.

The windows in the house were all wide open and his car which always sat at the end of the driveway in front of the garage was not there. John's heart sank. Something out of the ordinary must have happened. He couldn't remember anything of the sort in all the years of his coming home.

Taking his jacket in his hand, John covered the remaining hundred feet or so at a fast pace, almost running, and called out his wife's name when he reached the driveway. Then, although she couldn't have answered him so quickly, he called out the names of his son and daughter, and, no longer waiting for an answer, ran toward the side of the house to the door that led to the kitchen. It was open, with only the screen door shielding the interior from the outside. The former looked black, as if filled with water.

"Honey, where are you!?" John called out in a voice full of apprehension as he stepped inside but stopped still as he saw the kitchen was empty. All the furniture was gone from it and through the door leading to the dining room he saw that the latter was empty too.

All sort of explanations began competing with each other in his mind as to what might have caused this, but then his attention was drawn by a white sheet of paper lying on the kitchen counter next to the sink. It stood out sharp against the black Formica top, almost blinding him like a bright rectangular light.

Suddenly all quiet inside but conscious of a coherent if painful explanation forming itself in his mind, he walked up to the counter, put his briefcase down on the floor and the jacket on the counter, picked up the sheet of paper, and read what was written on it.

It said,

"Dear John,

"It has been building up inside me for years now and finally I can't take it anymore. I am leaving you and taking the kids with me. I am also taking most of the furniture. I am leaving you some of the furniture in the bedroom, including the bed, and that in your study. I can't tell you where we're going because with your wild temper you might do something to us. But don't worry about us. We'll be alright. You will hear from my lawyer in a few days, and we can start arranging for a divorce and disposal of the house.

"Take care of yourself and good luck.

Mary."

2.6.5 Rewrite the text from 2.6.4, stating in the beginning how the story will end and modifying the text appropriately to make it effective if necessary.

A Homecoming 2

The day his wife left him John stepped out of the train on his way home from the office as always at 5:30 sharp and the hands of the clock high up on the station tower dutifully pointed each to its proper spot on the dial, dead still, as if welded there for good. This was the only position he ever saw them in, being too rushed to check the clock in the morning. His house was less than a mile away and even if he walked at a leisurely stroll pace, as always again, he would be there by quarter to six.

He had what he believed to be a good marriage, with a devoted wife and two young kids, and there hadn't been any signs that something of the sort that awaited him at home was coming. Tired after a hard day's work, he looked forward to a restful evening in the peaceful surroundings of his home and family. The day was beautiful and warm for early May, and after walking for a few minutes John took off his jacket and carried it draped over his left arm to better enjoy the weather, while holding his briefcase in his right hand. He enjoyed feeling the balmy air on his skin as it pushed its way in through the fabric of his shirt. The sky was pale blue and clear, and only here and there little while clouds would scurry across it one after the other, jumping up and down and from side to side like railroad cars in an old suburban train carrying their passengers home after a day's work in the city. The cars nowadays were big and heavy and they charged thundering ahead, only the resting places of their final destination on their mind.

John thought of the strong little arms of his son and daughter which would wrap themselves around his neck as he would squat down to welcome them when he stepped into the driveway, of the smooth perfumed cheek of his wife which she would offer him for a kiss when he stepped into the kitchen, and the tasty supper he would be consuming in a matter of minutes, with all four of them seated at the dining room table, which she prepared to welcome him home with. Another couple of hundred feet and his house sprung into view—pale blue on the background of the dark green trees around it, as if an emissary of the sky above them. The grass of the immaculate lawn he toiled over each Saturday looked like a giant green wedge driven deep into the ground and the shadow of the huge sycamore tree next to the house resembled a giant black ball restring on the ground.

The windows in the house were all wide open and
his car which always sat at the end of the driveway
in front of the garage was not there. John's heart
sank. Something out of the ordinary must have
happened. He couldn't remember anything of the
sort in all the years of his coming home.

Taking his jacket in his hand, John covered the
remaining hundred feet or so at a fast pace, almost
running, and called out his wife's name when he
reached the driveway. Then, although she couldn't
have answered him so quickly, he called out the
names of his son and daughter, and, no longer
waiting for an answer, ran toward the side of the
house to the door that led to the kitchen. It was
open, with only the screen door shielding the
interior from the outside. The former looked black,
as if filled with water.

"Honey, where are you!?" John called out in a voice
full of apprehension as he stepped inside but
stopped still as he saw the kitchen was empty. All
the furniture was gone from it and through the door
leading to the dining room he saw that the latter
was empty too.

All sort of explanations began competing with each
other in his mind as to what might have caused
this, but then his attention was drawn by a white
sheet of paper lying on the kitchen counter next to
the sink. It stood out sharp against the black
Formica top, almost blinding him like a bright

rectangular light.

Suddenly all quiet inside but conscious of a coherent if painful explanation forming itself in his mind, he walked up to the counter, put his briefcase down on the floor and the jacket on the counter, picked up the sheet of paper, and read what was written on it.

It said,

"Dear John,

"It has been building up inside me for years now and finally I can't take it anymore. I am leaving you and taking the kids with me. I am also taking most of the furniture. I am leaving you some of the furniture in the bedroom, including the bed, and that in your study. I can't tell you where we're going because with your wild temper you might do something to us. But don't worry about us. We'll be alright. You will hear from my lawyer in a few days, and we can start arranging for a divorce and disposal of the house.

"Take care of yourself and good luck.

Mary."

Compare these two texts. Is either of them more effective than the other? What can you say about the two approaches?

The ending in "A Homecoming 1" should come as a complete surprise to the reader. In "A Homecoming 2" the ending is known from the beginning, but the reader doesn't know how it will happen. "A Homecoming 1," then, relies on surprise, while "A Homecoming 2" relies on suspense. Both seem to be equally effective in their own way, although some readers may prefer one to the other. It is up to the author to decide how he wants to impact the reader.

Comment: May there be a reason other than John's work schedule that he arrives at the station at 5:30? Try to find out on your own if you care.

2.6.6 Write a text with the action taking place in a dream.

Hunger 1

John dreams he is walking down a street, holding a dog on a leash. He doesn't particularly like dogs, doesn't own one now and hasn't owned any in the past, but feels reasonably well disposed toward the dog and feels he is fulfilling his duty. The dog is the size of a big boxer and, although it looks somewhat like a boxer, it is shaggy and has a bigger head. It is poorly groomed as if it were a stray dog and seems to be a mutt.

The dog is straining on the leash as if in a great hurry to get someplace or to find something and

John has a hard time holding it back by pulling as hard as he can on the leash. The collar must be choking the dog because it wheezes as it runs along but this doesn't prevent it from pulling forward as hard as it can. It doesn't even seem to notice what is happening. Its urge to move fast is stronger than its discomfort.

They are walking along the sidewalk and suddenly there is a dark mound of something in front of them. It looks like a pile of garbage that has somehow found its way there.

The dog sees the garbage and, as if crazed, rushes forward toward the pile, almost making him fall down on his face. He keeps his balance, however, and holds on to the leash.

There is a black plastic bag in the middle of the pile and the dog goes for it. Viciously, with its teeth bared, as if attacking another dog, it sinks it teeth into the bag and with a few tosses of its big head, rips it apart. Something big and green is inside it looking like a watermelon, and the dog sinks its teeth into it. It is in fact a watermelon. The dog is clearly very hungry and this was the reason it has been rushing so persistently ahead—it has been looking for something to eat. It is only then he notices how skinny the dog is—under the shaggy fur it is all skin and bones. It has been starved nearly to death. No wonder it is so hungry.

The dog has opened its mouth wide and has sunken its teeth into the watermelon as if wanting to swallow it whole. The latter is too big, however, for the dog to be able to do it. It tries to bite off a piece but has a hard time doing it. The watermelon looks hard. It must be frozen solid.

The dog keeps on trying to bite off a piece of the watermelon but is unable to do it. In the end, however, it opens its mouth so wide that it is able to take it all in. It is amazing that it can do it. It keeps jerking its head forward as famished dogs do eating and little by little the watermelon keeps on going deeper and deeper into the dog's mouth until it disappears inside it altogether. The dog makes a few more of these moves and then swallows hard and the watermelon goes inside its stomach.

He feels sick at the sight. He imagines what it must feel like to have a whole frozen watermelon in one's stomach. He is sure the dog will have a big problem digesting it. He will almost certainly get sick from it. Besides, he observes, it won't do much to still its hunger. Watermelons are virtually all water.

2.6.7 Write a text with the action taking place in real life which corresponds to the situation in the text in 2.6.6 (that is, for which the text in 2.6.6 is a symbolic representation).

Hunger 2

It is night. John has come home from work. He is
in his basement on the stairs leading into the
kitchen. It is dark all around him. The light switch
is on the wall by the door in the kitchen and there
is no corresponding one on the bottom to turn the
light on from there. When he was fixing up the
basement he decided not to put one in because it
would have cost too much. He has turned the
basement light by the side door off so as not to
have to come down later to do it.

He holds his briefcase in his left hand and with his
right one looks for the doorknob. He runs his palm
aimlessly over the smooth surface of the door for a
while and finally finds the doorknob. Its smooth
three-dimensional shape feels good in his hand
after the empty flatness of the door. John turns the
doorknob, pushes on it, feels the door open, climbs
up the two remaining steps, and finds himself in the
kitchen. Some light penetrates into it from the
outside and he can recognize the familiar shapes of
the stove, counter, and refrigerator. After total
darkness, they are also comforting.

John steps forward, turns right, walks a few steps
toward the wall, looks with his right hand for the
light switch on it that turns on the ceiling light,
finds it, and flips it. The space of the kitchen and
the objects in it spring into view as if physically
transporting themselves from someplace else. This

is likewise comforting to John and much more so
than on the other two occasions, although he
doesn't make this observation.

Normally he puts his briefcase away, changes his
clothes, and washes up before fixing his supper.
Tonight, however, he decides to fix his supper first.
He is too hungry. Besides, he doesn't feel like
walking into the darkness in the rest of the house.
He sees through the door on his right the dark
space of the dining room and knows what the rest
of the house would look like. He doesn't want to
tackle it now. He puts the briefcase on the floor
and goes to work.

He will fix himself scrambled eggs. He thought of
eating them with bread but he remembers that he
has run out of it so he will eat them alone. He
doesn't feel like fixing himself anything else to eat
the eggs with. He gets a skillet out from under the
counter, puts it on the stove, pours some olive oil
from a bottle standing on the window sill above the
sink into it, turns on the burner, gets two eggs from
the refrigerator, cracks them open, pours them into
the skillet, throws the eggshells into the sink, gets
a fork out from a drawer next to the stove, stirs the
eggs with it a few times, and stands watching the
clear egg white gradually turn white over the heat.
The eggs look forlorn all by themselves in the
skillet, so he decides to add some milk to them, as
if to keep them company. He gets a milk carton
out of the refrigerator, pours some milk into the

skillet, mixing the mixture in the process with the fork, puts the carton back into the refrigerator, and goes back to watching the eggs cook, stirring them from time to time.

The flame under the skillet is turned on too high and the eggs cook quickly, turning gradually into dry white lumps. Feeling they are done, John turns the fire off under the skillet and starts eating the eggs straight out of it, without taking it off the burner. It is too hot to be put on the counter and might damage the latter's top.

John eats with his pelvis pressed against the stove, his head bent down and his eyes unfocussed, mechanically transferring the eggs from the skillet to his mouth. They have no taste and if it weren't for their warmth it would be as if he were moving the fork aimlessly back and forth between the stove and his mouth. They are a big pale blur in the skillet below him and make him think of ruins he saw on his trip to Greece many years ago when he was young. He imagines marble would taste like they do if it were soft enough to eat.

Compare these two texts. Which of them is more effective? What advantages does each of them have over the other?

"Hunger 1" conveys an image of extreme type of abstract hunger applicable not only to animals but also to humans. "Hunger 2," on the other hand, is a realistic description of a man trying to assuage his hunger under which lies his feeling of loneliness. Both of the stories are effective in their own way. When resorting to the dream technique, the writer has the ability to create a more vivid, emotionally more powerful situation, freed from the restrictions of time, space, rules of physics, etc. So if this is the author's aim, he should resort to this technique. The realistic approach paints the picture of hunger which is easier for the reader to relate to. Also, if "Hunger 2" were part of a novel, it could show that the effect of some preceding event was an evocation of extreme loneliness and hunger in the character John; or/and that extreme loneliness and hunger in the character John had an impact on some subsequent event.

2.6.8 Write a "nonsensical" text in a free-association way on the model of automatic writing.

The heat sticky as flies. No wonder the clock makes that ticking sound. And the water dripping underneath. The water ticking like a clock. Its drops like the wheels in a clock. Transparent wheels. Cogwheels. Each drop already formed in the mass of water but you can't see it because they're transparent. Numbers in the water too. Lots of them crawling like ants. Transparent too. The meaning of numbers. Values of the digits. Hands covered with them. Like with short black hair. My hands in the water with invisible numbers on them. Drops clinging to them. Numbers.

Transparent numbers.

Is the text completely nonsensical? Can you write a completely nonsensical text?

Even though the sentences in the above text were written with the goal of making them unrelated, since they were composed sequentially and are thus associatively related, there does appear to be a thread of something common between them, and if the reader assumes that they are meaningful as a unit, he/she will be able to stitch together some sort of sense out of them, according to the best of his/her abilities. This is so because there seems to be something that may be called *the Interpretability Principle* common to all human beings which makes them want to assign a meaning to any linguistic string which has not been overtly labeled as nonsensical, unless they are expressly averse to doing it. It is probably this mechanism that lies behind people's ability to interpret metaphorical language. It is therefore unlikely that a text consisting of grammatically well-formed sentences or phrases can be completely nonsensical. For a text to be truly nonsensical, it probably must contain a large number of grammatically ill-formed strings.

2.6.9 Rewrite the text from 2.6.8, making changes in it to make it "coherent."

The heat sticky as flies. And so many of them on

the walls. They seem to like the heat. Each one like the tick-tock of the clock. And there's water dripping from the faucet underneath it. It's ticking too like a clock. Its drops must be like the cogwheels in a clock. Transparent cogwheels. Each drop already formed in the mass of water but you can't see it because they're transparent. There must be numbers in the water too. Lots of them crawling like ants. Transparent too. It must be just the meaning of the numbers. That is, the values of the digits. My hands are covered with them as if with short black hair. My hands in the water with invisible numbers clinging to them. Drops of water clinging to them. Numbers clinging to them. Transparent numbers.

Compare these two texts. What can you say about them?

The text of 2.6.9 picks up the associations inherent in the text in 2.6.8 and, by making them explicit, becomes at least somewhat more coherent.

2.6.10 Compose a text of an existing one by picking out sentences in it in random fashion.

Comment: Using *Molloy*, by Samuel Beckett, n-th sentence on n-th page, pages 1-9 (numbered 7-15 in the text, *Three Novels*, Grove Press, 1958 edition.]

I am in my mother's room. He comes every

Sunday apparently. It was two men unmistakably, one small and one tall. But now he knows these hills, that is to say, he knows them better. He certainly didn't see me, for reasons I've given and then because he was in no humor for that. Yes, it was on orange Pomeranian, the less I think of it, the more certain I am. There I am then, informed as to certain things, knowing certain things about him. It was my hat that I beflowered. For the wagons and carts which a little before dawn went thundering by, on their ways to marked with fruit, eggs, butter and perhaps cheese, in one of these perhaps he would have been found, overcome by fatigue or discouragement, perhaps even dead.

Compare this text to that in 2.6.8. Is it nonsensical?

Because the sentences in the text in 2.6.10 were not composed sequentially and therefore there is no associative connection between them, this text is harder to be interpreted than the text in 2.6.8, although it can't be excluded that it will remain nonsensical for all English language readers. In most likelihood, this will be a function of the reader's ability and attitude toward the text.   As was said above, it appears that a truly nonsensical text must contain a large number of grammatically ill-formed strings.

2.7 genre

Here the word "genre" refers to structurally different works.

2.7.1 Write a short text consisting of a self-contained story.

Dog

Suddenly, in the thicket of the crowd, John saw a girl, sixteen or so, straining to carry a huge brown suitcase which was literally pulling her down by her right arm to the ground. This was it! This was the chance he'd waited for! What luck! The suitcase is probably full of clothes that could be sold for a good price and perhaps even food he could avail himself off right away. Maybe she's going to college—now's the time when students are checking in for the fall semester, and maybe she's eighteen or even older and only looks so young—and is lugging lots of provisions her mother has prepared for her to take to school. He swallowed the saliva which had filled his mouth at the thought of the delicacies he would be savoring in a matter of minutes—roast beef, spicy meatloaf, scrumptious preserves, pound cake, chocolate chip cookies he hasn't tasted for years.... Nimbly, like an eel swimming between reeds, he slunk his way past the hurrying people and in a few seconds was next to the girl.

Here, let me help you, honey, he said in a sweet

voice, as he eased the girl's hand from the handle of the suitcase which she had gradually let sink to the floor.

She didn't understand what was happening at first, but then found an explanation and said in a soft breathy voice, looking up at him, Thank you so much.

Which way are you going? He asked as he lifted the suitcase and turned in the direction she'd been walking in. It felt heavy even for him, heavier than he had expected. No wonder the poor thing was having such a hard time with it.

Over there, the girl pointed with her hand ahead and to the right. The exit on that side.

OK, he said, let's go, and rushed off like a whirlwind toward where the girl had pointed.

She followed him after a few seconds' delay, but in a couple of steps fell further behind and continued doing so more and more. People were moving this way and that getting in his way, but he dodged them expertly, rushing as fast as he could and as he glanced over his shoulder after a few more seconds he couldn't see her. She didn't call after him either and that was probably because she expected he would be waiting for her at the door. So much the better!

Like a possessed eel now, he kept swerving around
the ever appearing obnoxious shapes getting in his
way, moving gradually more and more to the left
where he was sure the girl wouldn't follow him. The
suitcase was really heavy and he was getting out of
breath. Still he pushed on. He couldn't afford
permitting his body to let him down right now.
A wide corridor opened to his left, he turned the
corner and ran into it. He thought he heard
someone's voice behind his back calling out in
anger or despair. It was probably the girl having
realized what was happening. He had to get away
from her! He ran even faster, his feet slipping over
and over on the polished stone floor.

One more turn to the right, then another one to the
left, his heart was in his throat, but there was no
one yelling now behind him. He reached the door
leading outside, pushed it open, glanced over his
shoulder, there was no one behind him, he found
himself in the street, the door shut, he started
running to the left but saw the intersection in that
direction was far away, turned right, saw the
intersection was much closer there, ran toward it,
crossed to the other side as there were no cars
coming either way, ran down the street, made a
few more turns, and wound up in a dark narrow
alley with no one around.

There was a niche in the wall halfway down it on
the right—a blind doorway—and he put the suitcase
down there and stood, pressing against the wall so

as not to be seen and breathing heavily, barely able
to catch his breath. The suitcase huddled against
his leg like a faithful brown dog. Good boy, he
thought, barely able to stop himself from stroking
it, and glanced furtively out of the doorway in the
direction he had come from. There was no one
coming and momentarily no people walking down
the bigger street.

After a few minutes, when his breathing had gotten
back to normal, he decided to see what loot he had
earned his right to. He laid the suitcase on its side,
got down on one knee, opened the lock, and raised
the lid.

Instantly, like a jack-in the-box, he shot up, giving
out a scream that was a mixture of horror and fear.

Comfortably tucked in, inside lay on its side a big
brown shorthaired dog, as it looked a boxer. It
didn't stir and seemed sound asleep, indifferent to
what it had just been through and what awaited it.
For a few seconds John couldn't assign a meaning
to what he saw but then thoughts began to arrange
themselves into a coherent pattern. The dog was
dead. The girl was carrying it somewhere. She
couldn't have been carrying it home…. Most likely
someplace to dispose of it…. A dog cemetery… or a
crematory…. That is a vet…. There probably are no
pet crematories as such and you have to go
through a vet….

What a fool he'd been, he thought on. No, just bad luck.... How was he to know what was in the suitcase? Bad luck as always.... And speaking of bad luck, what would happen if someone found him with the dog now? Especially a policeman.... How would he explain himself?... And in the end would have to dispose of the dog or pay a fine.... Some mess he has gotten himself into! He had to get away! Right away! As fast as possible!
He was going to run in the direction he came from but decided it'd be wiser to go the other way. That street was relatively busy. Maybe the other one was less so. And, besides, he might run into the girl if he went back that way.

He took off, running, keeping his eyes on the pale smudge of brightness before him.

It was only then he realized what the girl must have thought after she realized what was happening. She probably stopped trying to catch up with him and stood there, her sides splitting with laughter. He must have only imagined she was calling after him. The only thing he could think of was, Oh, my God!

Give it more than one title and consider what impact each of them has on the story. Are they different? Which do you find the best? Why?

The conventional title for the story would be "Thief," since it would focus the reader's attention on the perpetrator of the crime, which is the subject of the story. It would certainly be appropriate but would not add anything to the story's effect. The reader would react to it in the same way if the story were left unnamed. "Dog" focuses the reader's attention on the grotesque ending, going beyond the nature of the crime of stealing. The mention of the imaginary brown dog rubbing against the thief's leg further stimulates the reader's attention, giving the story added depth. Another possible title could be "The Suitcase." It would be an attempt to turn the story into one of surprise, and would be appropriate for commercial writers such as O'Henry and Chekhov.

2.7.2 Write a text that constitutes a synopsis of an original work some 5-10 pages long.

Full Bath

There is no sink or bathtub in his bathroom so, to wash up, John either uses a basin when he washes just his upper body or the kitchen sink, into which he climbs in when he takes a full bath.

One day when he decides to take a full bath the sink is full of dishes he has been stacking up for almost a week, being too lazy to wash them. Not feeling like doing them at the moment, he stacks them up on the counter and on a nearby stool and climbs into the sink.

While washing himself, he slips and falls down, knocking over the dishes on the counter which in turn knock over those on the stool, and they all come crashing down onto the floor. While falling himself, John hits his chin on the edge of the stool and beaks a few teeth as well as cuts his tongue, and finally hurts his wrist on landing. In the end he lies there among broken dishes, nearly as smashed up as they.

Spitting out blood and teeth and cringing from the pain in his wrist John realizes he is seriously hurt and needs help. He lives alone, so he decides to seek help from his neighbors. He hasn't spoken to any of them since moving into the apartment years ago and is sure some of them think he is deaf-mute, but feels now is the time to break the habit. He has no choice. He only hopes they will respond in a friendly manner.

He gets up, grabs the towel he was going to dry himself with to cover himself up, and runs out into the corridor.

There are four apartments on the floor including his own. No one answers when he knocks on the doors of the two closest to his. It is too early in the afternoon and people are still at work. He comes home earlier than most people do. When he knocks on the third door, it is opened by the man who lives there. John knows him by sight, although they have never exchanged a word or even a nod. Beside himself with pain, John tries to explain to the man what has happened. To his surprise he discovers he can barely speak because of having hurt his tongue. Incomprehensible babble mixed with blood and bubbling saliva comes streaming out of his mouth. The man looks with terror and incomprehension at him. It is then John realizes he is stark naked. He must have dropped the towel as he was rushing out the door. Desperate to the extreme, John tries to explain to the man with gestures and mangled speech what has happened but it is to no avail. The man looks at him with bewilderment for a few more seconds and then, shaking his head and indicating he doesn't understand what John is saying, shuts the door in his face. It looks as though he really thinks John is deaf-mute. John understands why this is so and is sorry for his behavior in the past but it cannot be changed. The only thing for him to do is to go back to his apartment. When he tries to do that he discovers that the door is locked, however. He rushed out of it without releasing the latch. He stands there naked and bleeding from his mouth, not knowing what to do.

2.7.3 Write a synopsis of an original novel.

Crocodile Smiles

John's father worked at a municipal asphalt plant and his mother was a washerwoman. John was the couple's third and only surviving child. The previous two—a girl and a boy—died in their

infancy. John's mother couldn't heave any children
after him. She had tuberculosis and was ten years
older than her husband. The family lived in an old
tenement not far from where John's father worked.
Often left alone at home as a little child, John would
stand for hours on end at the kitchen window,
watching the flat industrial landscape stretching to
the horizon.

Smoke streamed out of the smokestacks sticking up
into the sky like long black hair and he imagined
himself a giant with a comb in his hand going
around, combing them to make them look prim.
Clouds chased each other in the sky like dogs, from
time to time getting into a vicious fight. Sometimes
he imagined his father coming out of the
smokestack of the plant where he worked like a
wispy cloud of smoke and waft over to the window,
and then turn into himself when he opened it to let
him in. This way he would be home sooner.
Later, when he went to school, John would often
skip classes and explore the world on his own.
He saw water running over the rapids in the river
that skirted the city. There was garbage of all sorts
in it caught in between the rocks. Once there was
the corpse of a little baby stuck there for a couple
of days before it was washed away. His mother
said it must have been thrown into the river by the
girl who'd given birth to it because she wasn't
married.

One morning he got up real early and saw the sun

rise out of the ground like a big red tulip already in bloom, ready to open up. He also watched for a few days a yellow tulip growing out of the ground on the edge of the garbage dump. When he came to see it one morning, someone had stepped on it and rubbed it out like a cigarette butt.

One day when he was in first grade the teacher took the whole class to the zoo. They saw there lions, tigers, giraffes, monkeys, snakes, and crocodiles. He liked the crocodiles the best because all they did was sit still with their mouths wide open smiling from ear to ear. They did this because they thought the world was great and they were happy in it. His father said those weren't smiles but something else, but he was sure they were smiles because what else could they have been if the crocodiles had their mouths full of big teeth open ear to ear without doing anybody any harm. He dreamt about the crocodiles that night and from time to time in the future without any apparent reason why.

His best friend became Joe, a boy who didn't go to school because he had no parents. He met Joe one day when skipping school and playing by the river. Joe showed him how to catch fish with his hands and squirrels in traps and roast them on open fire. They tasted great. Joe also took him to a place where girls went swimming naked. Joe said the girls would pee there sometimes in the open and it was fun to see, but it never happened when they were there. Joe taught him how to steal turnips out of a farmer's field, apples from an orchard, and fresh rolls from the baker's stand in the market. He tried to talk him into stealing money from the grocer cashier's drawer, but it was too scary. Joe laughed at him and called him a chicken but he still wouldn't do it. Something inside was stopping him which he couldn't overcome.

Once again, when he was much bigger, the teacher took them to a museum. There were many beautiful things there like pictures, sculptures, church things, and jewelry. He especially liked a diadem made of gold and studded with jewels which he thought of as a crown. He especially liked a diadem made of gold and studded with jewels which he thought of as a crown. He couldn't stop thinking about it and even had a dream in which he had found it in the street and gave it to a girl in his class he had fallen in love with. Her name was Maria, and she was the most beautiful girl in school, and all the boys were in love with her, but she paid no attention to any of them because she came from a rich family. She especially paid no attention to him which made him love her even more.

John told Joe about the crown and the latter said they could break into the museum at night and steal it and then he could give it to the girl and she would fall in love with him. John wouldn't agree to the idea at first, but as Joe kept urging him on to do it and Maria smiled at him one day during a recess, in the end he agreed.

They went over to the museum late one night and when they broke the window the watchman came running and Joe shot him with a gun he had brought along. He hadn't told John about it and John was shocked when it went off. The watchman was wounded but not badly and caught John, but Joe escaped. No one ever saw him after that. John was arrested, tried, and sent to a reform school for three years.

While John was in the reform school his father died. He fell into the pit where asphalt was mixed, was badly burned, and died soon thereafter.

When John got out of the school and went to where they lived he found the apartment locked. It turned out his mother had been taken ill two days earlier and was in the hospital. John went to see her but she was too sick to recognize him. He was told she didn't have much time left before she'd die.

When he went back home he was told he had to leave the place. They were being evicted for not having paid the rent for over a year. Their furniture was being confiscated as partial payment for what they owed on the rent but John was told he could take the rest.

He gathered up all the belongings, put them in the wheelbarrow his mother used to transport the laundry in from and to the clients, and left.

He didn't know where to go but followed the road into the city. To do this he had to cross the bridge. There was a lot of traffic in it, and it was hard for him to move. The wheelbarrow was heavy and the bridge sloped up toward the crest in the center. He still had no idea where he was going and for an instant thought of the zoo where the crocodiles lived. Back then, when he saw them, he would have thought this would be a good place for him to go to. Now, however, he knew better and pushed the thought out of his mind before it had time to fully form itself. All he could think was, if only he'd make it to the center of the bridge. It would be all downhill after that.

How does it differ from the one in 2.7.2?

The synopsis in 2.7.2 consists largely of a description of actions, whereas the one in 2.7.3, in addition to a description of actions, contains information about the background of the actions and environment in which they take place. This expands the scope of the narration, permitting the reader to imagine actions which haven't taken place but which may happen, involving the characters that have been described. In other words, the first synopsis describes an event, whereas the second one describes characters, who are generators of events.

2.7.4 Write the first and last paragraph of this novel.

First Paragraph

The first thing he remembered about himself was standing at the kitchen window in their apartment looking outside. His father was away working at the asphalt plant and mother had gone to pick up or drop off the laundry she did every day or was doing it at the clients' place. It was dead still in the building as most of the adults were away at work and kids in school, so the only thing he could do was watch the world outside. Tall thin smokestacks stuck up high into the sky all over the flat industrial landscape stretching to the horizon, smoke coming out of them blowing in the wind like long unkempt hair. He imagined himself a giant walking among them combing the smoke with a huge comb to make them look neat as his mother did combing his hair in the morning.

Last Paragraph

It was late morning and the traffic on the bridge was heavy, with buses, trucks, passenger cars, and horse-drawn wagons jostling each other while barely creeping along. He was in the middle of it, hemmed in on all sides like a splinter on the surface in a river among big logs during a spring flood, his arms hurting from holding up the handles of the heavy wheelbarrow, his lungs on fire from the effort, and his feet slipping on the smooth hard cobblestones with which the bridge was paved. It sloped up toward the crest in the center which he could barely see over the things piled up in the wheelbarrow as he stared wide-eyed ahead. He still had no idea where he was going and for an instant the memory of that sheltered enclosure in the zoo where he saw the crocodiles lying still with their mouths wide open when he was a little boy flashed through his mind. Back then he would have thought that was a good place for him to go to but now he knew better and pushed the thought out of his mind before it had time to fully form itself. The only thing he could think about was to make it to the crest of the bridge. It would be all downhill after that.

2.7.5 Write a synopsis of a film based on this novel.

Crocodile Smiles

The film is in black and white, in places deliberately silent, with or without subtitles, the images at times of deliberately poor quality. All actors are nonprofessional. Most important scenes:

John standing at the window as a little boy. Smokestacks with smoke streaming out of them, blowing in the wind. John imagining walking through the landscape and combing the smoke. John imagining his father coming out of the smokestack and wafting over to the window and he letting him in. Mother doing laundry. Father coming home from work and washing up in a basin on a stool next to the kitchen window. John in

school. John sees the sun rise. John watches a
tulip grow out of the ground on various occasions.
The tulip rubbed out by a foot.   The river. John
playing on the river bank. The rapids, beautiful in
places, full of garbage in others. John in school
again. John skipping school. The rapids with the
body of a baby in it. John speaking to his mother
about the baby, she explaining. John in school.
John skipping school and going to the rapids. The
body of the baby gone. The rapids beautiful, with
almost no garbage in them. John bigger. The visit
to the zoo. Crocodiles with their mouths open wide.
John mesmerized by the sight. Stays behind when
the class moves on. Has to be fetched. John
talking to his father about the crocodiles. John has
a dream about the crocodiles with him among
them. The crocodiles gentle and playful. He tries to
smile like them. John meets Joe. John and Joe on
the river on different occasions. Joe teaches John
to catch fish with his hands and to trap squirrels. A
similar crocodile dream. Joe and John roasting fish
and eating it. Roasting a squirrel and eating it.
Stealing turnips, and apples, and rolls from the
baker's stand in the market. Another similar
crocodile dream. Joe trying to convince John to
steal money from the grocer cashier's drawer. The
beautiful girl Maria. John falls in love with her.
Another similar crocodile dream. The visit to the
museum. John astounded by everything, especially
the diadem. John talks to Joe about Maria. John
reluctant to do it. Maria smiling at John.   John
telling Joe he agrees to break into the museum.

The museum grounds at night. The boys climbing over the fence, breaking the window. The watchman running. Joe shoots him. John aghast. Is caught by the watchman. The trial scene. John entering the reform school. A few scenes from the reform school. John is notified of his father's death. No reaction. A crocodile dream with crocodiles chasing him, trying to bite him. John leaves the facility. The tenement, locked apartment door. John talking to the superintendent. At the hospital. The mother unconscious. John back in the apartment. Spends the last night there. Half-empty kitchen in the moonlight. Gathers up the belongings in the morning and puts them into the wheelbarrow. Sets out toward the city. View of the city from across the river. John on the bridge jostled on all sides. View of the crest of the bridge over the things piled up in the wheelbarrow. A flash of the original image of the crocodiles. John stares straight ahead toward the crest at the center of the bridge. An expression of mad determination in his bulging eyes.

2.7.6 Write a review of this film.

Life Is Great for Crocs!

If you thought crocodiles don't show emotions, you should see *Crocodile Smiles,* which maintains—or at least its leading character does for a while—that they grin from ear to ear, showing how happy they are being alive.

The film, which is based on an obscure novel of the same name by MM, tells the story of a boy named John from the age of about three to around sixteen whose father works at the municipal asphalt plant and mother is a washerwoman working day and night to supplement her husband's meager wages. The family lives in a cramped apartment in a decrepit tenement on the edge of a large industrial city, not far from the plant where the husband works, apparently in the early to mid part of the twentieth century. Left alone at home, the boy stands all day long at the kitchen window watching the dreary landscape outside, daydreaming about being a giant who combs the smoke coming out of the smokestacks and welcoming his father back home as he floats over to the window in the form of a cloud of smoke

He grows up a dreamer who lives searching for beauty in life. When the schoolteacher in first grade takes his class to the local zoo he is enchanted by crocodiles resting with their mouths wide open, trying to cool off, and thinks they are gentle, peaceful creatures who do no harm to anyone in spite of their fearsome looks but lie all day on their stomachs smiling ear to ear, showing how happy they are with the world. John often cuts classes and meets a homeless street-wise boy named Joe who ultimately leads him astray. When the class is taken on a field trip to the local museum (he is around twelve or thirteen now), John falls in love with a golden diadem on display there which he dreams of giving to Maria, the most beautiful girl in the school who ignores him. While trying to break into the museum at night, the boys are surprised by the watchman whom Joe shoots with a gun he has secretly brought along. Joe escapes, but the slightly wounded watchman catches John who is sentenced to three years in reform school. While there John learns his father has been killed in an accident at the plant—he falls into the pit where asphalt is mixed. Thus John's childhood dream is fulfilled but he is not there to welcome his father home.

When John is released, he discovers they are being evicted from their apartment for nonpayment of rent and his mother is in the hospital. She is on the verge of dying and doesn't recognize John when he comes to see her. The family's furniture is confiscated as partial payment for what is owed on the rent and John loads up the remaining possessions into the wheelbarrow his mother used to transport laundry in and sets out toward the city. To get there he has to cross the bridge and as he is stuck in the traffic on it a thought flashes through his mind he should go to the zoo where the crocodiles live to stay with them. Knowing better now, he dismisses the thought, however, and pushes on, struggling up the upward curving bridge, reaching out with his maddened eyes for the still distant crest in the center as if it were all downhill for him after that.

The film is shot in often scratchy but sometimes painfully sharp black-and-white reminiscent of the Italian neorealist cinema of the 1940's. It also frequently resorts to the silent film technique which is used here to excellent effect. NN, the director as well as the author of the script, camera man, and editor has created for us an amazing work of art which is bound to move the viewers, astound the critics, and set the art of cinematography on the road it should have taken long time ago. The stellar acting—living, one should rather say—is by exclusively nonprofessional actors whose names for the time being have been withheld. The most amazing is the character of John. He is played by four different boys, each of whom in a particular age stage looks exactly as the one who played in the preceding age stage would be expected to look. How this is accomplished is not clear—was NN able to find a family with four brothers of the required ages who looked so much alike, or did he just happen to come across four unrelated boys with such amazing resemblance? Or is it that the film was made over a period of some thirteen years with the same boy playing all the roles? It is unthinkable that likeness to this degree could have been accomplished with simple makeup. This will remain a mystery until the question is answered when the names of the actors are made public. When this will happen we don't know, as Mr. N has so far refused to make it clear.

But perhaps it is better this way. Hurry up, and see this amazing film when it still appears to be life itself.

2.7.7 Write a text which constitutes the description of a fragment from this film which depicts one or more objects.

Half-Empty Kitchen in the Moonlight

A small square window in the wall, the frame forming a cross, its four arms of equal length. Moonlight coming into it at an angle, making the dirty windowpane look like cobwebs rather than glass. A plain rectangular wooden table at an angle to the window and some three feet away from it. Limp gray shadows cast by the edges of the table like thick tattered cobwebs hanging all the way down to the floor. The floor littered with dust balls, dry bread crusts, scraps of other food, bits of paper, and so on, a bent worn aluminum soup spoon among them. A small white gas range and an also small and white partitioned kitchen sink like frightened children huddling against the wall on the right. The kitchen otherwise empty.

Through the cobweb-like pane can be barely made out a flat industrial landscape with dark single-storied structures and tall, thin smokestacks sticking up sharply into the cloudless sky as if to cause it harm. The moon perfectly round but small, seeming afraid to get closer to the earth.

2.7.8 Write a text which constitutes the description of a fragment from this film which depicts action.

Breaking into the Museum

White walls of a large two-storied building with dark windows partly hidden by black, shadow-like trees seen through straight, tall bars of an iron fence. The space illuminated by distant street lamps and perhaps moonlight filtered through thin clouds. Joe followed by John steal up on tiptoes to the fence, the first carrying two long poles held together and the second something looking like small partly filled sack or a cushion. Joe separates the poles and it is clear that they are joined by rows of thick rope which constitute the rungs of a ladder. He leans the ladder against the top of the fence, digs the bottoms of the two poles into the ground, and slowly climbs up the rungs. The poles tend to move together but stay apart far enough for him to be able to move up. When he is close to the top, he reaches down with his right hand toward John and the latter gives him the object he has been carrying. It turns out to be a sack filled with something soft but firm. Joe takes the sack and lays it over the tops of the bars of the fence, climbs higher, slides with his body over the fence with the sack under him, and jumps down to the ground, crouching as he does that. John follows Joe, proceeding in exactly the same fashion. Once there, the boys maneuver the ladder to their side of the fence between its bars and set it up for them to

get back out. The sack remains in the same spot
on top of the fence.

The two boys, now once again walking on tiptoes
but this time hunched over, move in the direction of
the building, Joe first, and John following. At first
their footsteps are quiet, as they walk on grass, but
then light crunching is heard as they tread on the
gravel with which the ground around the building is
covered. Having reached the building, they stop by
the nearest window. It is perhaps four feet off the
ground and they can easily reach it. John sticks his
right hand into his pants pocket, pulls out a big
rock, and gives it to Joe who stands closer to the
window. The latter glances at it, then looks
cautiously around, turns his head back to the
window, and with a sudden sharp move hits the
windowpane with the rock, making it break. A loud
melodious sound is heard as the glass shatters,
followed by silence. Joe quickly looks around once
again and then turns his head back and starts
hitting the glass sticking in the frame, trying to get
rid of all of it, clearly so that they would be able to
climb inside.

The sounds are less melodious now and are
accompanied by dull ones when the rock hits the
wood of the frame. They continue as Joe keeps
clearing the glass away.

A loud scream is then heard, followed by the sound
of feet thumping on the ground, coming from the

left, which grow progressively louder, indicting it is someone running toward the boys from that direction.

John yells at Joe, "Stop!" Joe realizes what is happening, stops hitting the window, and looks to his left. A figure of a man dressed in a dark uniform is seen running along the wall, hunched over and gesticulating with his hands. John huddles against the wall behind Joe, the latter throws the rock in the direction of the man which misses him, reaches inside his waistband, and pulls out a small revolver. John looks aghast as he sees it; apparently he didn't know Joe had brought it along.

Joe points the revolver at the man who is now some ten feet away from him and fires.

A dry cracking sound is heard like a stick breaking and smoke rises from the barrel of the revolver and its chamber.

The man hesitates slightly as if having been shot somewhere on his body, but continues moving forward, his arms outstretched, toward the boys, yelling something as he runs. He has now almost reached them.

Joe drops the revolver, turns around, and runs as fast as he can in the direction they have come from, disappearing in the darkness under the trees

and leaving John alone. He is huddling hunched up
and frightened against the wall.

The man reaches him, grabs him by the shoulders
with both hands, turns him around, and presses
him firmly against the wall. There is an expression
of not so much fear as profound amazement on
John's eyes.

*2.7.9 Rewrite the story of the novel in 2.7.3 in the
form of a short letter to someone familiar.*

Dear Mary,

Wanted to tell you about this novel I've just read.
It's by a writer I've never heard of—MM. Started it
last night and finished this morning as it was
getting light. Couldn't put it away. It's called
"Crocodile Smiles." It's about a boy who thinks that
crocodiles are gentle creatures who smile ear to ear
because life is great for everyone, until the very
end, when he finally realizes what life is really like.
He saw them once in a zoo on a school trip sitting
with their jaws wide open, trying to cool of, and
thought they were smiling. He's called John and
lives in a decrepit tenement building with his
mother and father. The mother is ten years older
than her husband and does laundry for other
people, and the father works at the municipal
asphalt plant nearby. The boy turns into a dreamer
as he stands at the window all day alone in the
apartment, watching the world outside. Later, when

he goes to school, he becomes friends with a homeless boy named Joe who leads him astray by enticing him to break into a museum to steal an expensive diadem he saw on another school visit to give it to a girl he's fallen in love with. During the break-in Joe shoots the museum guard but runs away, while John is caught and is sent to a reform school for three years. When he gets out, his father is dead (he fell into the asphalt pit at the plant and was burned alive) and the mother is sick at the hospital. She's been in poor health all her life and the recent tragic events were too much for her to bear. John finds this out when he comes home and discovers further that they are being evicted from the apartment for nonpayment of rent. He visits his mother at the hospital but she's in a coma and doesn't recognize him. He's permitted to spend one more night at the apartment but must leave in the morning. The furniture and other things of value are confiscated as partial payment on the rent, and John loads up what's left of their belongings in the wheelbarrow his mother used for transporting laundry in and goes away. He doesn't know where he's going but as he's stuck in traffic on the bridge leading into the city he remembers the zoo where he saw the crocodiles years ago and decides he certainly isn't going there. He recalls that at one time he would have thought that was a good place to go to.

You must read this book. It's a treasure. I'll send it to you in a few days. I just want to look through it a few more times to make sure I haven't missed anything.

Hugs and more,

John

Compare the texts in 2.7.3, 2.7.5, 2.7.6, and 2.7.9. What can you say about them? Was one of them easier to write than others? If so, then why?

Four different views on a physical object contribute to its description and understanding, since new information about the object is added by each. This isn't true of four takes on the same subject such as those above. They all present the same overall view of the topic, but select different features which to highlight. The synopsis has the full store of facts and makes all of them available to the reader. The latter can choose to arrange them in any order of importance he/she desires. The film director/script writer has chosen the features of the story best suited for visual representation. The reviewer of the film concentrates on those aspect of the film that permit him/her convey the desired message to the reader. And the author of the letter speaks of what it is that has made him like the book the most.

The four texts do show, however, how one can deal with a topic in four fundamentally different ways. Each has its own style and each evokes different reaction in the reader. It is this fact that is being brought to the student's attention here. The lesson to be learned is that taking a different stance toward a topic will result in a different text, in which different aspects of the story will be given different emphasis. It is for the writer to decide what he/she wants to present to the reader.

As to the ease of writing—in this particular case none of the four texts appeared to be easier to write than the others, with the film review being a possible exception. (It may have been the ebullient title of the piece which opened the gates of the author's imagination to flow exceptionally freely.) But one might suspect that for most students the letter form would be the easiest to compose. This would be so because this form permits the writer to act naturally and does not put up any artificial demands on his/her writing. It is these which are most probably the primary cause of the difficulties writers frequently face which are known as "writer's blocks."

Comment: The epistolary novel form has not been given attention in this book but, for the reasons just stated, it is advisable for the student to get acquainted with this genre. A good work from which to start the study of it is the classic *Les Liaisons dangereuses [Dangerous Liaisons]* by the 18th century French novelist Pierre Choderlos de Laclos.

2.7.10 Write an anecdote, making it as brief as

possible.

Name Change

A man named John Shitt comes before a judge and asks for his name to be changed, "for obvious reasons." The judge examines the name and readily agrees. What would he like it to be changed to? he asks.—Spell it with one "t," please, the man replies.

2.7.11 Write a few concise epigrams

1. The world is always whiter on the other side of the skin.
2. The skin is closer to the flesh than the shirt.
3. Would the violet bloom more beautifully if it knew how the rose does it?

Discuss them.

Epigram 1 speaks of the natural tendency of people to think that those different from them are better off. It is a racially motivated paraphrase of the well-known saying that grass is always greener on the other wide of the fence.

Epigram 2 speaks of the difficulty of people to be fair to others in light of their natural tendency to be positively disposed toward their own.

Epigram 3 suggests one should remain true to

oneself and not try copying others.

All three epigrams are based on metaphors. That is, they speak of concrete physical situations which in an allegorical fashion refer to abstract phenomena. It appears that their effectiveness, whatever it may be, stems precisely from this characteristic. Consider for instance, a "nonmetaphorical" paraphrase of Epigram 3— "Always be yourself and don't try copying others." It says the same thing as the original but it is without doubt less effective.   It shouldn't be assumed, however, that epigrams must always be built on metaphors. It seems to be safe to say, however, that there must be something in their language which distinguishes them from everyday speech, for instance, brevity, rhythm, rhyme, alliteration, and so forth. Consider the Latin saying "*Mens sana in corpore sano,*" which strikes one with its lapidary nature and the repetition of the stem "*san.*" The "*ns*" in "*mens*" is probably of negligible importance.

2.7.12 Write a scholarly or scientific article.

Explanation of why Boiling Water Freezes Faster Than Cold

Phenomenon

Given two identical vessels A and B containing the same quantities of water, the one in A being cold and the one in B boiling, when placed in an environment whose ambient temperature is below freezing, the water in B will freeze sooner than that in A.

Process of Freezing

Water in a vessel freezes from the outside toward the inside. If the vessel is a cylinder open on top, the water will freeze on top first and, assuming the material from which the cylinder is made is a good conductor of heat, e. g., a metal like copper, it will then freeze from the sides and bottom of the cylinder toward the inside, eventually freezing solid all the way through, assuming the ambient temperature of the environment is cold enough and the vessel is left in it sufficiently long. Now, since water is a poor conductor of heat, and definitely so in its frozen state (note the use of ice in constructing dwellings by inhabitants of very cold regions), it will take a long time for the innermost reservoir of water to freeze solid. When the ambient temperature of the environment is not very much below 0 °C, this might not happen at all if the vessel isn't permitted to stay in the cold long enough.

Explanation of the Phenomenon

When the water in the vessel is cold, e.g., a few degrees above 0 °C, the process will proceed as outlined above, with very little, if any, movement of water in the vessel. The freezing will commence as the temperature of the outermost layer of water drops to about -2 °C, at which point the water will turn to ice. When the temperature of the ice (in reality originally a mixture of ice and water) drops below -2 °C, the temperature of the layer of water touching the ice will start dropping and eventually this layer will freeze in the same fashion as the preceding one. In this way all the water in the vessel will proceed freezing until it is frozen all the way through.

When the water in the vessel is hot (boiling), its outermost layer will be cooled first, causing its density and thus specific gravity to rise. The denser and thus heavier water will sink to the bottom, causing the warmer, less dense and thus lighter water to rise. This will give rise to a continuous movement of the water in the vessel, with the warmer water flowing to the top and the outside of the vessel and cooler to the bottom and inside. Ultimately the temperature of the water in the vessel will reach a near uniform approximately -2 °C, and will continue freezing uniformly throughout the vessel, with crystals of ice being carried from the top and outside of the vessel toward its inside. This will no longer be due to the difference in the specific gravity of the different layers of water however but to the momentum of the currents generated earlier. At some point though, the movement of water will cease and the freezing will then proceed in the fashion outlined above for cold water, but apparently the overall time of freezing will still be shorter than in a case when there was no appreciable movement of water from the start. This must be due in part to the fact that every object loses heat in an inversely exponential fashion, that is, exponentially slower and slower, and in part to the insulating effect of frozen water mentioned above.

What can you say about the language in the text in 2.7.12 as compared to that in the texts in 1.3, 2.7.1, and 2.7.4?

The language in the text in 2.7.12 is a highly structured, virtually artificial language that closely adheres to the pattern normally used in writing of this sort and is devoid of any emotional coloring. The language in the poems in 1.3 and the fiction texts in 2.7.1 and 2.7.4, on the other hand, show none of these characteristics. Although the particular texts in these three sections don't show the full spectrum of language that can be used in them, there are few, if any, restrictions on it. The kind of language used in such texts as those in 1.3 may appear in such texts as those in 2.7.1 and 2.74 and the other way around. It may also include the type of language used in 2.7.12, especially in the case of the fiction texts. The reverse cannot be said about the language in the text in 2.7.12, however. Although the rules of syntax and rhetorical pattern in it do permit variation, the scope of these is limited and no emotionally charged vocabulary or constructions are typically permitted.

In connection with the topic of strictness of language, note the rigid, formulaic language used in the statement of the exercises in this book. Care was taken to use identical expressions in intentionally similar situations so as not to suggest differences where none exist. Natural languages contain virtually no true synonyms, for even when different linguistic strings have the same denotation (refer to the same object or concept), they typically carry different connotation (emotional, stylistic, etc. implication) and thus mean something else.

2.8 structure

The aim of these exercises is to show different ways of structuring a work of fiction.
2.8.1 Write a synopsis of an original novel based on a plot (chronological development of a story). It should be a smoothly flowing narration. You can use the synopsis from 2.7.3 if the novel you wrote about falls into this category.

Comment: Using *Crocodile Smiles* from 2.7.3.

Plot is sometimes understood in its narrowest definition, as a necessary causal relationship between successive events, each indispensable for the next one, so that in the chain of events *a, b, c...z, a* is the primary cause of *z*. Generally, however, this restriction is relaxed so that a mere chronological relationship between successive events, so long as they are related in some reasonable fashion, is sufficient for them to be considered as part of the plot. This is closer to Aristotle's definition of plot, where the "necessary" causal relationship restriction is eased by the added stipulation "or probable."

Actually, in *Crocodile Smiles,* the relationships between virtually all events, or "stages," described in the synopsis are causal in at least a subtle way. The essential characteristic of John is that he is born into a poor family and that his mother is of ill health. Because of the former, he is forced to be alone as a child and turns into a day dreamer, craving for beauty, which he misses in his oppressive urban surroundings. Because he searches for beauty, he meets Joe, whose behavior he confuses with his own search for beauty. Craving for beauty also makes John fall in love with Maria, and falling in love with the diadem, being under the influence of Joe and Maria's smiling, causes him to take part in a crime for which he is severely punished even though his role in it is secondary. Because his parents are poor, the father ultimately loses his life, and because the mother is of ill health to start with, she dies before he grows up, and he becomes a homeless orphan in the end. According to the story, then, the final outcome was inevitable, given the two original conditions. Thus, poverty and ill health of a parent are the cause of suffering and ultimate homelessness and orphanage of John. The introduction of the crocodile image is an ironic element aimed at heightening the painfulness of the story.

2.8.2 Write a synopsis of an original novel based on a principle other than chronology or plot, e.g., location, characters, type of action, period of time, etc. You can use the synopsis from 2.7.3 if the novel you wrote about there falls into this category. Unlike the text in 2.8.1, this will not constitute a smoothly flowing narration, but will be an enumeration of facts, features, events, actions, etc. There will have to be some criterion which will bind them into a whole, however.

Apartments

The novel is a description of apartments 411, 412, and 413 in the tenement at 400 Granite Street and the story of the people who live in them. It is divided into three parts, one for each of the apartments, each named with the apartment's number.

Each part is organized in the following fashion: appearance of the bedroom, view from the bedroom window, furniture in the bedroom, appearance of the kitchen, view from the kitchen window: furniture in the kitchen, appearance of the bathroom, furniture in the bathroom, name, status, gender, and age, of each inhabitant, followed by the description of each inhabitant and his/her story, which constitutes the bulk of the text for the part.

All apartments are located on the fourth floor, are of the same size, and consist of a bedroom, kitchen, and bathroom.

Apartment 411

Bedroom: dirty dull white peeling walls; outside flat industrial landscape stretching to the horizon, smokestacks with wispy hair-like smoke streaming in the wind, factories with serrated roofs like saws threatening the low gray sky; three identical narrow beds, a big brown wardrobe, a black chest of drawers chipped in places, showing white paint underneath, a red rickety chair. Kitchen: dirty shiny white walls; a small dirty white gas range, a small divided sink next to it, a small white counter with cabinets next to it, a white rectangular wooden table, three red chairs; view the same as from the bedroom window. Bathroom: dark, no window, dirty peeling shiny white walls; a toilet bowl with a black seat, no sink. Inhabitants: Robert Black (27) husband, Mary Black (25) wife, Peter and Paul Black (4) identical twin sons.

Robert Black: short and wiry, with sunken usually unshaven cheeks and short black hair. Poor working class family background, grade school

education, works at the municipal asphalt plant.
Lost both of his parents as a teenager. Passionate
about horse racing. Goes seldom to the races
because of the cost, but bets frequently, small
amounts most of the time, occasionally winning.

Mary Black: Small, thin, flat-chested, with a plain
face and mousy hair. High School education.
Comes from a relatively well-to-do family. Very shy
and quiet, an indifferent homemaker, an obedient
wife, and a devoted mother. Unlikely as it seems,
is thought by some to be having an affair with
Richard Schuster from apartment 413.

The two boys similar like two drops of water.
Delicate, faces, without any resemblance to either
of the parents. Both stutter heavily. The parents
have been assured the boys will get over it when
they grow up. Sleep in the same bed. The parents
sleep in separate beds because of the mother's
constant twitching in her sleep.

Apartment 412

Bedroom: dirty dark green walls; view of building at
401 Granite Street, four floors tall, flat roof with
smoke stacks, stained dark gray stucco walls, some
windows open, other closed, some with curtains,
other without, narrow courtyard below littered with
paper, garbage, about half a dozen boys playing in
it; a double bed with a matching wardrobe, the
veneer cracked and peeling on the latter, and a

matching dresser with an oval mirror in somewhat
better condition, a small matching chair next to it, a
picture of Jesus on The Mount of Olives above the
bed, a cot covered with a gray blanket in the
corner. Kitchen: shiny green walls; a small dirty
white gas range, a small divided sink next to it, a
small white counter with cabinets next to it, a small
rectangular white table with two matching chairs
next to it; view the same as from the bedroom
window. Bathroom: dark, no window, peeling shiny
green walls; a toilet bowl with a white seat, no sink.
Inhabitants: Luciana Sciavone (67), Vincent
Sciavone (43) her son.

Luciana Sciavone short, heavy, bow-legged, with
sagging breasts and gray hair, widow of Luigi
Sciavone, a worker at the municipal asphalt plant
who died 17 years ago at the age of 62 of natural
causes, lives off he husband's pension. Comes
from the same village in Calabria, Italy as her
husband, who emigrated years earlier, came back
to look for a bride, and married her without having
known her before. (She was a child when he left).
The couple had three sons, but lost the two older
ones (Joseph and Anthony) in the war. Vincent, the
youngest one, tall, thin, dark, an invalid, lost his
right leg in a job-related accident at the railroad
company he worked for 16 years ago, lives off the
pension he receives. Prefers crutches to his
prosthetic leg, which he uses seldom, and only for
special occasions. Seldom shaves. An alcoholic.
Harbors secret erotic emotions toward Astrid

Schuster from apartment 413.

Apartment 413

Bedroom: Clean white walls; the view the same as that from the windows in apartment 411. All furniture looking new and custom-made from white pine. A double bed and a three-tier cot in the corner. A big wardrobe, a chest of drawers, and a small desk with two chairs next to it. Full-color magazine clippings of Mediterranean-looking landscapes neatly framed on the walls. Kitchen: shiny white walls; a small white gas range, a small divided sink next to it, a counter with drawers underneath and a cabinet above it matching the furniture in the bedroom. A long table with six chairs along it likewise matching the furniture in the bedroom; view the same as from the bedroom window. Bathroom: dark, no window, shiny white walls; a toilet bowl with a white seat, no sink but a small standing cabinet with a white enameled basin on top of it.   Inhabitants: Joseph Schuster (31), Astrid Schuster (29), Anna Schuster (7), Barbara Schuster (5), Christine Schuster (3), Diane Schuster (2).

Richard Schuster: tall, thin, attractive, blond hair and blue eyes. Some High School education. A carpenter, together with his older brother Rudolph co-owner of a carpenter shop. An attentive father and husband. At times shows jealousy, toward his wife without any cause. Was considered to be a ladies man before he got married.   Still appears to be vulnerable to female charms. As was said, is rumored by some to be involved with Mary Black from apartment 411.

Astrid Schuster: dark-haired, shapely, very attractive, born in Sweden, comes from a poor immigrant family, some High School education, a devoted wife and mother.

The four daughters all blond, pretty, looking more like their father than mother, the eldest in first grade.

Comment: The well-known novel *La Vie mode d'employ (Life: User's Manual)* by the Oulipo author Georges Perec is constructed on a similar principle.

2.8.3 Rewrite, or describe how you would rewrite, the text from 2.8.1, basing it on some nonchronological principle as defined in 2.8.2. What did you have to do to achieve this? What difficulties did you run into in your attempt?

Since the tightly-structured plot part of *Crocodile Smiles* (the museum break-in scene) is straight-forward, it would be easy to rewrite it as a narration of the event in which each chronologically preceding act (the cause) is not presented as the impetus for the successive one (the effect), but as a mere statement of fact, for instance, something along the lines, "John got caught by the watchman when he was trying to break into the museum together with Joe, who shot the man with a gun he had brought and then escaped." But we would still be left with a chronologically structured work which would retain same of its plot-type flavor. So, in addition to the suggested rewriting of the scene, the whole story of John would have to be reorganized in some other fashion. One way of doing this could be to segmentize John's life and classify it into pleasant (beautiful) and painful (ugly) events and present them separately. These could be listed in chronological order without imparting a taste of plot to the work. The "beautiful" part would contain such scenes as John at the kitchen window, John seeing the sun rise, clean rapids, the crocodile scene, Maria, the diadem in the museum, and so forth; the "ugly"—the stamped-out tulip, the corpse of the baby, being caught during the break-in, the reform school, news of the father's death, in the hospital, and so on, ending with the scene on the bridge. (Here the crocodile scene would finally take on its "ugly" nature.) But this version of the novel almost definitely would not be as effective as the original one, since there is nothing in the story which would justify structuring it this way; it would not be artistically convincing. In other words, the *Crocodile Smiles* story seems to lend itself best to the chronological, plot-based structure. One must not exclude, however, the possibility that there are stories which can be told equally effectively both ways.

2.8.4 Rewrite or describe how you would rewrite the text from 2.8.2, basing it on a plot. What did you have to do to achieve this? What difficulties did you run into in your attempt?

As it has been described in 2.8.2, *Apartments* may be characterized metaphorically as a cross-section of part of the fourth-floor of the tenement at 400 Granite Street and of the life of the people who live there. The picture is fully static; time in it has been frozen and turned into a substance (events of the past). There are points in it, however, which could be of use if one wanted to turn it into a plot-based work.

The three apartments are interconnected through supposed or real relationship between some of the their inhabitants—Mary Black of apartment 411 may be having an affair with Richard Schuster from 413, and Vincent Sciavone of apartment 412 is secretly in love with Astrid Schuster from apartment 413. In the new novel, the static part of the story—the description of the three apartments and the background of all the inhabitants—could be left unchanged, where it would serve as a background of the developing story, as it was frequently done in the introductory parts of 19th century novels, and then a tight-plot section could be added, elaborating in detail the interplay between the affected characters. For instance, it may be Vincent who is the driving force in the plot part. Burning with a passion for Astrid, he senses that there may be something going on between Mary and Richard, spies on them, and discovers that his suspicion was justified. He sets a trap for them, they fall into it, he makes Astrid witness to what is going on between her husband and Mary, which leads to the denouement. It could be tragic or ironic—Robert kills Mary and Astrid kills Richard, or conversely, Robert leaves Mary and the children, and Astrid stays in the marriage, accepting Richard for what he is. In either case Vincent's dream of getting Astrid doesn't come true—he remains a crippled lonely bachelor as he had been before wrecking both marriages or the one of the family in apartment 411.

Notice that here new material had to be added to turn the "static" novel of 2.8.2 into a plot-based one. This could have been avoided if the background of the inhabitants in *Apartments* of 2.8.2 had included the events described here, that is, if Robert had already killed Mary and Astrid had killed Richard, or if Robert had left Mary and the children and Astrid has accepted Richard's infidelity and stayed in the marriage. But here, the events would have been described in the form of a tightly-structured plot rather than as static events that took place in the past.

2.9 subject

The aim of these exercises is to improve the

technique of developing subject and imagination. 2.9.1 Write a synopsis of a work based on a well-known subject—e.g., the Agamemnon cycle, the legend of Tristan and Isolde, the story of Raskolnikoff, etc.—replacing one or more essential elements of the original with new ones. In the Agamemnon cycle, for instance, the essential element is the unjust and insidious revenge of one person over another and its tragic consequences. In the legend of Tristan and Isolde, the essential element is the prohibition of illicit love and the latter's inevitable tragic end. In the Raskolnikoff story, the essential element is a horrific crime and the feeling of guilt it evokes which leads to a voluntary acceptance of punishment. Write a synopsis of the original work first and then that of your version.

Agamemnon Story, Original

Helen, the wife of Menelaus, the king of Sparta and younger brother of Agamemnon, the king of Mycenae, is abducted by Paris, son of the king of Troy Priam, and taken for his wife. Incensed, the mainland Greeks form an army led by Agamemnon to free Helen and punish Troy. They gather with their boats on the Boeotian shore in Aulis and wait for propitious winds to take them to Troy and carry out their task. The air is dead still for a long time, however, pestilence descends on the waiting troops, and it is discovered through the soothsayer Calchas that this is the punishment of the goddess

Diana for Agamemnon having killed her favorite
stag while hunting. She will relent if Agamemnon
sacrifices for her his maiden daughter Iphigenia.
Reluctant at first, Agamemnon consents to the
request out of a feeling of duty, sends for Iphigenia
to come under the pretext she will be married to
one of his brightest generals, the famous Achilles,
but during the sacrifice rite Iphigenia is enveloped
in a cloud and taken by the goddess to Tauris and
made a priestess in her temple, leaving a body
looking like that of Iphigenia in her place.

The Greeks finally sail to the shores of Asia Minor
and sack Troy after many years of siege. Menelaus
gets back his wife, each of the Greeks receives his
proper share of the bounty, which for the generals
includes the women of the Priam household, and, to
everyone's surprise, Agamemnon who, as the
commander-in-chief, can have his pick of anyone,
chooses Priam's youngest maiden daughter
Cassandra in spite of her considered to be mad; she
is said to be capable of foretelling the future. He
finds her so beautiful that he can't resist having
her.

Agamemnon makes Cassandra his concubine and
returns with her to Mycenae where Cassandra and
Agamemnon's cousin Aegistus in the meantime
have become lovers. The two plan Agamemnon's
murder. Cassandra warns Agamemnon of the
danger awaiting him but he pays no attention to
her, convinced she is mad. Clytemnestra and

Aegistus kill Agamemnon while he is taking a bath and afterwards do the same to Cassandra.

Agamemnon Story, Variation 1

The same as the original through Agamemnon's getting Cassandra as his prize.

As he gets to know her during their first night together, Agamemnon discovers that Cassandra isn't mad but possessed of extraordinary poetic gifts which sometimes make her capable of predicting the future. They fall in love with each other and become lovers.

Upon returning to Mycenae, the two continue their relationship, flaunting it in front of everyone, including Clytemnestra who grows very jealous, in spite of having in the meantime entered into a relationship with Aegistus. Cassandra warns Agamemnon of the danger they are facing, but Agamemnon dismisses them as untrue, feeling that at times she can be wrong.

Clytemnestra and Aegistus plan the couple's murder and Agamemnon and Cassandra are killed by the two as the former make love while taking a bath.

2.9.2 Write a synopsis of the text in 2.9.1, replacing one or more essential elements of the original with different ones.

Agamemnon Story, Variation 2

The same as the original up to the destruction of Troy.

Diana wants to punish Agamemnon more than she has let on. She makes Iphigenia look like Cassandra and substitutes her for the latter, without Iphigenia realizing what is going on. Agamemnon and Pseudo-Cassandra become lovers as in Variation 1. Agamemnon finds out Clytemnestra has been unfaithful to him and kills her as well as Aegistus with the help of Pseudo-Cassandra. While Agamemnon and Pseudo-Cassandra make love celebrating what they have done, Iphigenia regains her likeness and awareness of herself and the two realize what they have been doing. Iphigenia commits suicide and Agamemnon tears his eyes out and goes wondering through the world as a beggar.

2.9.3 Write a synopsis of the text in 2.9.1, replacing one or more essential elements of the original with still different ones.

Agamemnon Story, Variation 3

The same as the original through the couple's arriving in Mycenae.

Agamemnon finds out Clytemnestra has been unfaithful to him, kills her and Aegistus with the help of Cassandra, and the two rule Mycenae together.

Compare these three texts. How do they differ?

Variation 1 dilutes the original tragic nature of the story by introducing the element of love between Agamemnon and Cassandra, making Clytemnestra's action at least partly justifiable. Variation 2 not only retains the story's tragic nature but makes it even more tragically gruesome and because of this perhaps less effective. Variation 3 turns the original tragic story into one with a happy ending totally negating its power.

2.9.4 Write a synopsis of a mininovel, as the term has been defined in literature (Yuriy Tarnawsky, "The Mininovel and Negative Text," American Book Review, *May-June, 2007, reprinted in Yuriy Tarnawsky,* Claim to Oblivion, *JEF Books, 2016.), in other words a short work of fiction that relies on negative text (primarily omission of vital information), which is based on a well-known novel and which retains the intent and effect of the original. Limit your work to deleting information, without adding any vital information of your own. Write a synopsis of the original novel first and present your work in terms of it.*

Comment: Using *L'Etranger [The Stranger]* by Albert Camus.

Synopsis of the Novel

Part One

Chapter I. Thursday. Meursault goes by bus from Algiers to Marengo, to attend his mother's funeral. She had lived in the Old People's Home there and died that day. He doesn't look at the body and shows no emotions. Has coffee. He likewise shows no emotions next day at the funeral.

Chapter II. Saturday. Meursault is back in Algiers. Goes to the beach, meets Marie Cardona. They swim, go to the movies, then to his place, and spend the night together there. She is gone in the morning when he wakes up. He spends the Sunday alone.

Chapter III. Monday. Meursault is back at the office, busy. Dinner at Celéste's restaurant. Meets his friend Raymon Sintès. Writes a letter for him to entice the latter's girlfriend to come back so that he can humiliate her.

Chapter IV. Next Sunday with Marie. Raymond beats up his girlfriend. Her brother wants revenge.

Chapter V. Sunday with Marie. Agrees to marry her without enthusiasm.

Chapter VI. Next Sunday with Marie and Raymond at the latter's friend's beach house. Raymond is attacked by his girlfriend's brother and an Arab friend. Meursault goes walking on the beach alone with Raymond's revolver. The Arab is there. He flashes his knife at Meursault, who is disoriented by the strong sunlight, feels threatened, and shoots the Arab, killing him with the first shot and then fires four more.

Part Two

Chapter I. Meursault is arrested and a lawyer is assigned to defend him. The lawyer indicates his case is simple and he should be acquitted. During an interview with the magistrate Meursault's inability to have emotional feelings and his unnatural forthrightness become apparent.

Chapter II. Meursault in prison, in his cell. A visit from Marie. Gets a letter from her. Misses freedom. But these feelings subside and he gets used to being a prisoner. Lives on memories, sleeps.

Chapter III. Months go by. The trial. Meursault's inability to feel is brought up and he is depicted as a monster.

Chapter IV. Meursault is found guilty and is sentenced to death by the guillotine. He has nothing to say when given the opportunity to speak by the judge.

Chapter V. The verdict has been appealed.

Meursault refuses to see the prison chaplain three times. The chaplain comes to see him on his own. Tries to convince him to turn to God. Meursault gets angry and attacks the chaplain, explains how meaningless life is since there's always the certitude of death in the end. The jailers rush into the cell, free the chaplain, and he leaves with tears in his eyes. Meursault calms down, thinks about his upcoming death, and opens his heart "to the benign indifference of the universe."

Synopsis of the Mininovel 1

Chapter 1. Meursault has coffee at his mother's wake.

Chapter 2. Meursault's behavior at the funeral.

Chapter 3. Meursault at the beach with Marie and later in his apartment.

Chapter 4. Meursault alone on Sunday.

Chapter 5. Meursault kills the Arab.

Chapter 6. Meursault's interview with the magistrate.

Chapter 7. Meursault in prison, waiting for the trial.

Chapter 8. The trial.

Chapter 9. Meursault attacks the chaplain and is left alone.

Discuss your work by comparing it with your own synopsis of the original novel.

The mininovel retains the general thrust of the novel by stressing Meursault's alienation without going into the background of the killing of the Arab. It is explained in terms of the absurdity of life he describes in his last harangue.

2.9.5 Repeat the exercise of 2.9.4 for the same novel, changing to some degree the intent and effect of the original.

Synopsis of the Mininovel 2

Chapter 1. Meursault has coffee at his mother's wake.

Chapter 2. Meursault's behavior at the funeral.

Chapter 3. Meursault at the beach with Marie and later in his apartment.

Chapter 4. Meursault writes a letter for Raymond.

Chapter 5. Raymond beats up his girlfriend.

Chapter 6. Meursault with Marie and Raymond at the beach house.

Chapter 7. Raymond gets attacked.

Chapter 8. Meursault kills the Arab.

Chapter 9. Meursault's lawyer assures him he will be acquitted.

Chapter 10. Meursault in prison, waiting for the trial.

Discuss your work by comparing it with your own synopsis of the original novel.

This version concentrates on the killing, showing it to be justifiable at least to some degree, but leaves the reader uncertain as to Meursault's fate.

2.9.6 Write a synopsis of an original mininovel, paying special attention to crafting the negative text.

Comment: Rewriting *Crocodile Smiles* as a mininovel.

Synopsis of the Mininovel

1. John as a child, daydreaming at the kitchen window.
2. John's father washing up in the kitchen after coming home from work.
3. John playing by the river.
4. The crocodile scene.

5. John and Joe roasting fish by the river.
6. John beaten up by classmates in the schoolyard.
7. John stealing a roll from the baker's stand.
8. John watching Maria in the school yard during the recess.
9. The museum trip.
10. Dream about giving the diadem to Maria.
11. The trial and conviction.
12. John's first day in the reform school.
13. Dream about his father coming home as a cloud of smoke.
14. John at the apartment after returning from the reform school.
15. John at his mother's bedside in the hospital.
16. The final scene on the bridge.

Compare the three results. How do they differ?

The mininovel in 2.9.4 is essentially a condensed, "Reader's Digest" version of the novel, with little negative text, and therefore does not have much evocative power, as is expected of a mininovel. This is due to the fact that the effort was limited to deleting scenes from the original, which in this case made it difficult to create an effective negative text. The mininovel in 2.9.5 is a bit more effective because it leaves Meursault's future uncertain, forcing the reader to try to create one or more versions of it on his/her own. This was possible because the mininovel was made different in its intent and effect from the original work. The situation with the *Crocodile Smiles* mininovel is different. It is not a result of a mere deleting of scenes from an existing novel, as was the case with the preceding two, but an original work, where the text of each chapter has been written with the form of the mininovel in mind. Furthermore, additional new scenes, including two dealing with dreams, have been introduced into the story, to make the work more effective. Omission of the break-in scene and a hint at John's father's death without specifying its nature creates two powerful negative texts which the reader will have to fill in according to his/her abilities.

3. drama

The aim of these exercises is to develop the technique of writing a play. They are based on the assumption that a play is a work of fiction with clearly delineated spatial and temporal limits (the space of the stage and the viewer's patience, respectively). It may include common prose texts (conversations, narrations) as well as poems.

The word "text" appearing in the exercises below has the same connotation as in the exercises dealing with prose, with the understanding that it is designed to be performed on the stage.

3.1 elements

This is what plays are made up of.

Although composed independently, the texts produced in these exercises should be conceived as parts of a unified work—a play some 2-5 pages long. The order of the composed scenes may be rearranged at the end to produce the final work.

3.1.1 spoken text

3.1.1.1 Write a text consisting exclusively of a dialog between two people.

Comment: This text and all that follow is a highly condensed and modified version of Euripides' *Electra*.

El: Is that water I hear splashing?
Or: The quiet waters of the Styx roiled up by our hatred.
El: That will come later. Now it's the warm arms of the bath lulling them into half-sleep, to ease our task.
Or: Our accomplice, fourth co-conspirator.
El: It was their third one eight years ago.
Or: Yes, it put its soft palms tightly over our father's eyes.
El: Monstrous nature, evil villain, helping out where it can to see us writhe in pain at its feet, no matter who we are.
Or: Shhhh! The splashing has stopped. They may hear us.
El: No, I hear her giggling…. Him speaking.
Or: Planting seeds of lascivious words in her ears.
El: To come up as screaming babies out of her womb.
Or: Usurpers of our rights, who'll laugh at our rags, sic dogs on us to tear our bodies.
El: Shhhh! Don't speak so loud. They may hear us. They're all quiet now.
Or: Only the water splashes rhythmically.
El: As it did with our father.
Or: In that mad girl's arms.
El: We must get ready! The time has come.
Or: It's now!

3.1.1.2 Write a text consisting exclusively of a conversation between more than two people.

El: You're just in time. Have you got it?
Py: Yes. It's just the right kind. Here, take it.
Or: It's not too thick? Won't blunt the sword?
Py: No. It's meant for small fishes. Old too...
frayed... torn in places.... The sword will easily cut
through it.
El: But they won't tear it?... Free themselves?
Py: No, it'd be too hard. It'd take too much time.
Or: I... the sword... won't give it to them. See how
eager it is to do its work? Like a horse dancing in
one spot, ready to go... neighing and rearing up....
Two stabs and they're done.
El: Two won't be enough. They'll need more.
Or: They'll get more! Many more! One apiece will
be for starters... to let their bodies taste the
sword... its sharp flavor. Then they'll feast on it....
Have their fill.... Till they throw up... the red vomit
of their blood.
El: Shhhh! Enough rejoicing! Don't celebrate
before the time has come. Act first!
Py: Act, then dance with joy. Go! Go! The time
has nearly passed you. Act now!
El: Let's go!

3.1.1.3 Write a text consisting exclusively of a narration by one person, describing an action.

Py: Aeg turns his head left. There's utter surprise
on his face. Incomprehension. He doesn't

understand what's happening. Cly's face is turned right. Her eyes are huge. They're about to pop out of their sockets. She knows what's happening. A second more and she'll know who the young man is, although the last time she saw him he was a little boy. In a couple of steps El and Or are by the bathtub. They toss the net over the couple. It covers them like a mother's loving body a child. Aeg tries to free himself. Tries to stand up. Or lifts the sword in both hands high above his head. Plunges it down with all his might into Aeg's curving back. It sinks half in. Aeg gasps. Sinks down into the water. Or struggles to pull the sword out. Succeeds. Cly screams his name, Orrrr! Noooo! Now she knows who he is! Aeg's body shields her. Or tries to find a spot where to strike. Pushes Aeg away with his foot. El helps him. She grabs Aeg's hair through the net. Pulls on it. Exposes Cly's face and chest. Cly screams, Orrrr! Ellll! Noooo! Noooo! Noooo! Or plunges the sword into her mouth. It comes out easily. Or stabs Cly over and over again. In her neck, chest. Aeg stirs. Tries to get up. Or plunges his sword into his neck. Then the back. Over and over again. He's spluttered with blood. There's blood everywhere. The bathtub is a cauldron of boiling blood. The floor around it is covered with a tattered blood rug. There're fancy blood tapestries on the gray granite walls. Or turns around. His eyes are two flaming torches. His sword falls limp out of his hand. He stumbles forward. Reels from side to side as he walks. A soft whine like a thin stream of steam escapes from his mouth. El follows a few steps behind him, watching his progress. There's profound surprise on her face. She didn't expect this. None of us did.

Comment: Note that this is the way important action in a story was represented in Ancient Greek Drama.

3.1.1.4 Write a text consisting exclusively of a narration by one person, describing something other than action.

Or: Aaaaaaaaaaaaaaaa…. Aaaaaaaaaaaaaaaa…. Aaaaaaaaaaaaaaaa…. Killer of his own mother…. Aaaaaaaaaaaaaaaa…. Avenger of his father's death…. Aaaaaaaaaaaaaaaa…. Murderer…. Aaaaaaaaaaaaaaaa…. Avenger murderer…. Who will forgive me?... Who'll punish me to ease my guilt?... Aaaaaaaaaaaaaaaa…. Where will I find peace?... Where will I find a place where I'm not myself?... Aaaaaaaaaaaaaaaaaaaaaaaaaaaa….

3.1.2 behavior

3.1.2.1 Fill out the text in 3.1.1.1 with a description of how the people behave as they talk.

El and Or hunched over, huddling against the door.

El *(in a half-whisper, pressing her ear to the crack in the door):* Is that water I hear splashing?

Or *(also in a half-whisper, moving his head close to that of El while staying by the door)*: The quiet waters of the Styx roiled up by our hatred.

Both continue speaking in the same manner, their bodies glued to the door.

El: That will come later. Now it's the warm arms of the bath lulling them into half-sleep, to ease our task. *(Leans away from the door.)*
Or *(pressing his ear to the crack now)*: Our accomplice, fourth co-conspirator.
El: It was their third one eight years ago.
Or: Yes, it put its soft palms tightly over our father's eyes.
El *(angry):* Monstrous nature, evil villain, helping out where it can to see us writhe in pain at its feet, no matter who we are.
Or *(in a whisper, pressing the index finger of his left hand to his lips and leaning away):* Shhhh!
The splashing has stopped.   They may hear us.
El *(moving closer to the door without pressing her ear to it, in a whisper, as Or):* No, I hear her giggling…. Him speaking.
Or *(straightening up):* Planting seeds of lascivious words in her ears.
El *(not changing her position):* To come up as screaming babies out of her womb.
Or *(louder, seething with anger, shaking the sword in his upraised hand):* Usurpers of our rights, who'll laugh at our rags, sic dogs on us to tear our bodies.
El *(worried, pressing her ear to the crack in the*

door again): Shhhh! Don't speak so loud. They may hear us. *(After a pause.)* They're all quiet now. Or *(moving his head closer to El's, trying to listen):* Only the water splashes rhythmically.
El: As it did with our father.
Or: In that mad girl's arms.
El *(tearing herself away from the door, standing up straight, determined):* We must get ready! The time has come.
Or *(standing up as El, even more determined than she):* It's now!

3.1.2.2 Fill out the text in 3.1.1.2 with a description of how the people behave as they talk.

At that instant Py comes out of the darkness between the columns, carrying something tied in a bundle. El sees him and turns to him. Or does the same. Py comes up to the two.

El *(anxiously, in a whisper):* You're just in time. Have you got it?

The three huddle together by the door. Py spreads the bundle in his hands. It turns out to be a fisherman's net.

Py *(in the same kind of voice):* Yes. It's just the right kind. Here, take it. *(Gives the net to Or.)*
Or *(examining the net as best he can in the darkness, in the same kind of whisper):* It's not too thick? Won't blunt the sword?

Py: No. It's meant for small fishes. Old too...
frayed... torn in places.... The sword will easily cut
through it.
El *(anxiously):* But they won't tear it?... Free
themselves?
Py: No, it'd be too hard. It'd take too much time.
Or: I... the sword... won't give it to them.
*(Brandishes the sword while pressing the net to his
chest with the other hand.)* See how eager it is to
do its work? Like a horse dancing in one spot,
ready to go... neighing and rearing up.... Two stabs
and they're done.
El: Two won't be enough. They'll need more.
Or *(louder, brandishing the sword still more):*
They'll get more! Many more! One apiece will be
for starters... to let their bodies taste the sword... its
sharp flavor. Then they'll feast on it....   Have their
fill.... Till they throw up... the red vomit of their
blood.
El *(pressing her index finger to her lips):* Shhhh!
Enough rejoicing! Don't celebrate before the time
has come. Act first!
Py *(emphatically, but still in a whisper):* Act, then
dance with joy. Go! Go! The time has nearly
passed you. Act now!
El: Let's go!

*Or quickly unwinds the net, gives one end of it to
El, holds on to the other, the two rush to the door
and hurl themselves against it, making its two
wings fly open wide with a loud crash. Py runs after
them, but stops in the doorway and remains there,*

still as a statue, watching what is going on inside.

3.1.2.3 Fill out the text in 3.1.1.3 with a description of how the person behaves as he/she talks.

Py *(in a loud yet calm voice, staring straight ahead, but turning his head right from time to time and speaking to the audience over his shoulder on the background of the screams and sounds of the splashing of water coming from backstage):* Aeg turns his head left. There's utter surprise on his face. Incomprehension. He doesn't understand what's happening. Cly's face is turned right. Her eyes are huge. They're about to pop out of their sockets. She knows what's happening. A second more and she'll know who the young man is, although the last time she saw him he was a little boy. In a couple of steps El and Or are by the bathtub. They toss the net over the couple. It covers them like a mother's loving body a child. Aeg tries to free himself. Tries to stand up. Or lifts the sword in both hands high above his head. Plunges it down with all his might into Aeg's curving back. It sinks half in. Aeg gasps. Sinks down into the water. Or struggles to pull the sword out. Succeeds. Cly screams his name, Orrrr! Noooo! Now she knows who he is! Aeg's body shields her. Or tries to find a spot where to strike. Pushes Aeg away with his foot. El helps him. She grabs Aeg's hair through the net. Pulls on it. Exposes Cly's face and chest. Cly screams, Orrrr! Ellll! Noooo! Noooo! Noooo! Or plunges the sword into her mouth. It comes out easily. Or stabs Cly over and over again. In her neck, chest. Aeg stirs. Tries to get up. Or plunges his sword into his neck. Then the back. Over and over again. He's spluttered with blood. There's blood everywhere. The bathtub is a cauldron of boiling blood. The floor around it is covered with a tattered blood rug. There're fancy blood tapestries on the gray granite walls. Or turns around. His eyes are two flaming torches. His sword falls limp out of his hand. He stumbles forward. Reels from side to side as he walks. A soft whine like a thin stream of steam escapes from his mouth. El follows a few steps behind him, watching his progress. There's profound surprise on her face. She didn't expect this. None of us did.

Py steps out of the doorway, making room for the two to pass, then turns right and follows them with his eyes.

3.1.2.4 Fill out the text in 3.1.1.4 with a description of how the person behaves as he/she talks.

Out of the doorway comes Or, followed by El a few steps behind him, both covered head to toe with blood. Or moves slowly forward, pushing his feet on the floor without lifting them like a blind man afraid to fall down. His arms hang limp along his sides and his face is blank.

Or *(without emotion, barely audibly)*:
Aaaaaaaaaaaaaaaa…. Aaaaaaaaaaaaaaaa….

Aaaaaaaaaaaaaaaa…. Killer of his own   mother….
Aaaaaaaaaaaaaaaa…. Avenger of his father's
death…. Aaaaaaaaaaaaaaaa…. Murderer….
Aaaaaaaaaaaaaaaa…. Avenger murderer…. Who
will forgive me?… Who'll punish me to ease my
guilt?… Aaaaaaaaaaaaaaaa…. Where will I find
peace?… Where will I find a place where I'm not
myself?… Aaaaaaaaaaaaaaaaaaaaaaaaaaaa….

*He reaches the edge of the stage, falls down on his
knees, and collapses with his face on the floor and
arms thrown out before him. El falls on her knees a
few feet behind and to the side of him and stares
vacant-eyed at his prostrate body. Py watches the
two from the distance, an expression of
helplessness on his face.*

3.1.3 setting and character description

*3.1.3.1 Write a text consisting of the description of
the stage in the above texts.*

*A hallway or a corridor with an unusually low
ceiling, crowded, like a forest with dense-growing
trees, with short sturdy granite columns that seem
a Neanderthal version of tall slender marble ones
common in ancient Mediterranean architecture. The
air between them brown like water in a muddy
river. Black profile of low craggy hills in the
distance in the space between the columns with a
cold white light forcing its way up from behind them*

like a shucking knife opening a stubborn oyster shell. It must be the moon trying to rise. A two-winged, low, wide wooden door studded with black forged iron nails, house right. The door shut.

3.1.3.2 Write a text consisting of the description of the people in the above texts.

The three characters—El, Or, and Py—young, also short and sturdy, Neanderthalean-looking. El (female) with long dark hair, matted and unkempt, dressed in a long sleeveless dress made out of coarse brown sacking, tied with a thick rope around the waist. Or and Py (both male) with short likewise unkempt and matted hair, dressed in sleeveless tunics of the same coarse brown sacking as El's dress, reaching to the middle of their thighs, likewise tied with a thick rope around the waist. All three barefoot. In spite of the difference in gender, the three looking like identical triplets. Or carries a long, sharp copper sword in his hand which at times shines red, as if covered with blood.

3.1.3.3 Put the texts produced in 3.1.2.1, 3.1.2.2, 3.1.2.3, 3.1.2.4, 3.1.3.1, and 3.1.3.2 together, making changes when necessary to produce a unified text, and give it a name.

Comment: Putting the scenes together in the above order, while moving the descriptions to the front and calling the play "The Avengers."

The Avengers

A hallway or a corridor with an unusually low ceiling, crowded, like a forest with dense-growing trees, with short sturdy granite columns that seem a Neanderthal version of tall slender marble ones common in ancient Mediterranean architecture. The air between them brown like water in a muddy river. Black profile of low craggy hills in the distance in the space between the columns with a cold white light forcing its way up from behind them like a shucking knife opening a stubborn oyster shell. It must be the moon trying to rise. A two-winged, low, wide wooden door studded with black forged iron nails, house right. The door shut.

The three characters—El, Or, and Py—young, also short and sturdy, Neanderthalean-looking. El (female) with long dark hair, matted and unkempt, dressed in a long sleeveless dress made out of coarse brown sacking, tied with a thick rope around the waist. Or and Py (both male) with short likewise unkempt and matted hair, dressed in sleeveless tunics of the same coarse brown sacking as El's dress, reaching to the middle of their thighs, likewise tied with a thick rope around the waist. All three barefoot. In spite of the difference in gender, the three looking like identical triplets. Or carries a long, sharp copper sword in his hand which at times shines red, as if covered with blood.

Scene 1

El and Or hunched over, huddling against the door.

El *(in a half-whisper, pressing her ear to the crack in the door):* Is that water I hear splashing?
Or *(also in a half-whisper, moving his head close to that of El while staying by the door):* The quiet waters of the Styx roiled up by our hatred.

Both continuing speaking in the same manner, their bodies glued to the door.

El: That will come later. Now it's the warm arms of the bath lulling them into half-sleep, to ease our task. *(Leans away from the door.)*
Or *(pressing his ear to the crack now)*: Our accomplice, fourth co-conspirator.
El: It was their third one eight years ago.
Or: Yes, it put its soft palms tightly over our father's eyes.
El *(angry):* Monstrous nature, evil villain, helping out where it can to see us writhe in pain at its feet, no matter who we are.
Or *(in a whisper, pressing the index finger of his left hand to his lips and leaning away):* Shhhh! The splashing has stopped. They may hear us.
El *(moving closer to the door without pressing her ear to it, in a whisper, as Or):* No, I hear her giggling…. Him speaking.
Or *(straightening up):* Planting seeds of lascivious words in her ears.

El *(not changing her position):* To come up as screaming babies out of her womb.

Or *(louder, seething with anger, shaking the sword in his upraised hand):* Usurpers of our rights, who'll laugh at our rags, sic dogs on us to tear our bodies.

El *(worried, pressing her ear to the crack in the door again):* Shhhh! Don't speak so loud. They may hear us. *(After a pause.)* They're all quiet now.

Or *(moving his head closer to El's, trying to listen):* Only the water splashes rhythmically.

El: As it did with our father.

Or: In that mad girl's arms.

El *(tearing herself away from the door, standing up straight, determined):* We must get ready! The time has come.

Or *(standing up as El, even more determined than she):* It's now!

Scene 2

At that instant Py comes out of the darkness between the columns, carrying something tied in a bundle. El sees him and turns to him. Or does the same. Py comes up to the two.

El *(anxiously, in a whisper):* You're just in time. Have you got it?

The three huddle together by the door. Py spreads the bundle in his hands. It turns out to be a fisherman's net.

Py *(in the same kind of voice):* Yes. It's just the
right kind. Here, take it. *(Gives the net to Or.)*
Or *(examining the net as best he can in the
darkness, in the same kind of whisper):* It's not
too thick? Won't blunt the sword?
Py: No. It's meant for small fishes. Old too...
frayed... torn in places.... The sword will easily cut
through it.
El *(anxiously):* But they won't tear it?... Free
themselves?
Py: No, it'd be too hard. It'd take too much time.
Or: I... the sword... won't give it to them.
*(Brandishes the sword while pressing the net to his
chest with the other hand.)* See how eager it is to
do its work? Like a horse dancing in one spot,
ready to go.... Neighing and rearing up.... Two stabs
and they're done.
El: Two won't be enough.   They'll need more.
Or *(louder, brandishing the sword still more):*
They'll get more! Many more! One apiece will be
for starters... to let their bodies taste the sword... its
sharp flavor. Then they'll feast on it.... Have their
fill... till they throw up...the red vomit of their blood.
El *(pressing her index finger to her lips):* Shhhh!
Enough rejoicing! Don't celebrate before the time
has come. Act first!
Py *(emphatically, but still in a whisper):* Act, then
dance with joy. Go! Go! The time has nearly
passed you. Act now!
El: Let's go!

Or quickly unwinds the net, gives one end of it to

*El, holds on to the other, the two rush to the door
and hurl themselves against it, making its two
wings fly open wide with a loud crash. Py runs
after them, but stops in the doorway and remains
there, still as a statue, watching what is going on
inside.*

Scene 3

Py *(in a loud yet calm voice, staring straight ahead,
but turning his head right from time to time and
speaking to the audience over his shoulder on the
background of the screams and sounds of the
splashing of water coming from backstage):* Aeg
turns his head left. There's utter surprise on his
face. Incomprehension. He doesn't understand
what's happening. Cly's face is turned right. Her
eyes are huge. They're about to pop out of their
sockets. She knows what's happening. A second
more and she'll know who the young man is,
although the last time she saw him he was a little
boy. In a couple of steps El and Or are   by the
bathtub. They toss the net over the couple. It
covers them like a mother's loving body a child.
Aeg tries to free himself. Tries to stand up. Or lifts
the sword in both hands high above his head.
Plunges it down with all his might into Aeg's curving
back. It sinks half in. Aeg gasps. Sinks down into
the water. Or struggles to pull the sword out.
Succeeds. Cly screams his name, Orrrr! Noooo!
Now she knows who he is! Aeg's body shields her.
Or tries to find a spot where to strike. Pushes Aeg

away with his foot. El helps him. She grabs Aeg's hair through the net. Pulls on it. Exposes Cly's face and chest. Cly screams, Orrrr! Ellll! Noooo! Noooo! Noooo! Or plunges the sword into her mouth. It comes out easily. Or stabs Cly over and over again. In her neck, chest. Aeg stirs. Tries to get up. Or plunges his sword into his neck. Then the back. Over and over again. He's spluttered with blood. There's blood everywhere. The bathtub is a cauldron of boiling blood. The floor around it is covered with a tattered blood rug. There're fancy blood tapestries on the gray granite walls. Or turns around. His eyes are two flaming torches. His sword falls limp out of his hand. He stumbles forward. Reels from side to side as he walks. A soft whine like a thin stream of steam escapes from his mouth. El follows a few steps behind him, watching his progress. There's profound surprise on her face. She didn't expect this. None of us did.

Py steps out of the doorway, making room for the two to pass, then turns right and follows them with his eyes.

Scene 4

Out of the doorway comes Or, followed by El a few steps behind him, both covered head to toe with blood. Or moves slowly forward, pushing his feet on the floor without lifting them like a blind man afraid to fall down. His arms hang limp along his sides and his face is blank.

Or *(without emotion, barely audibly)*:
Aaaaaaaaaaaaaaaa….   Aaaaaaaaaaaaaaaa….
Aaaaaaaaaaaaaaaa…. Killer of his own   mother….
Aaaaaaaaaaaaaaaa…. Avenger of his father's
death….   Aaaaaaaaaaaaaaaa…. Murderer….
Aaaaaaaaaaaaaaaa….   Avenger murderer…. Who
will forgive me?...   Who'll punish me   to ease
my guilt?... Aaaaaaaaaaaaaaaa…. Where will I find
peace?... Where will I find a place where I'm not
myself?...   Aaaaaaaaaaaaaaaaaaaaaaaaaaaaa.

*He reaches the edge of the stage, falls down on his
knees, and collapses with his face on the floor and
arms thrown out before him. El falls on her knees a
few feet behind and to the side of him and stares
vacant-eyed at his prostrate body. Py watches the
two from the distance, an expression of
helplessness on his face.*

3.2 manner

*The aim of these exercises is to show the impact of
the manner in which a story is told on the audience.*

*3.2.1 Assuming the behavior of the characters in
the play developed in 3.1.3.3 was realistic, rewrite
the latter, replacing the behavior of one or more
characters in it with nonrealistic action which better
conveys the nature of the situation, changing other
elements if necessary. For instance, if a character
was talking about something painful, he/she might*

be made carry a heavy object. Such action, in this context, might be labeled as metaphorical, related in a counterpoint fashion to the spoken words. If the person was described as crying, the action would be labeled as an illustration, relating to it as one part to another in musical harmony.

Comment: Rewriting Scene 3 and Scene 4.

The Avengers
(Nonrealistic Version)

A hallway or a corridor with an unusually low ceiling, crowded, like a forest with dense-growing trees, with short sturdy granite columns that seem a Neanderthal version of tall slender marble ones common in ancient Mediterranean architecture. The air between them brown like water in a muddy river. Black profile of low craggy hills in the distance in the space between the columns with a cold white light forcing its way up from behind them like a shucking knife opening a stubborn oyster shell. It must be the moon trying to rise. A two-winged, low, wide wooden door studded with black forged iron nails, house right. The door shut.

The three characters—El, Or, and Py—young, also short and sturdy, Neanderthalean-looking. El (female) with long dark hair, matted and unkempt, dressed in a long sleeveless dress made out of coarse brown sacking, tied with a thick rope around the waist. Or and Py (both male) with short

*likewise unkempt and matted hair, dressed in
sleeveless tunics of the same coarse brown sacking
as El's dress, reaching to the middle of their thighs,
likewise tied with a thick rope around the waist. All
three barefoot. In spite of the difference in gender,
the three looking like identical triplets. Or carries a
long, sharp copper sword in his hand which at times
shines red, as if covered with blood.*

Scene 1

El and Or hunched over, huddling against the door.

El *(in a half-whisper, pressing her ear to the crack
in the door):* Is that water I hear splashing?
Or *(also in a half-whisper, moving his head close to
that of El while staying by the door):* The quiet
waters of the Styx roiled up by our hatred.

*Both continuing speaking in the same manner, their
bodies glued to the door.*

El: That will come later. Now it's the warm arms of
the bath lulling them into half-sleep, to ease our
task. *(Leans away from the door.)*
Or *(pressing his ear to the crack now)*: Our
accomplice, fourth co-conspirator.
El: It was their third one eight years ago.
Or: Yes, it put its soft palms tightly over our
father's eyes.
El *(angry):* Monstrous nature, evil villain, helping
out where it can to see us writhe in pain at its feet,

no matter who we are.

Or *(in a whisper, pressing the index finger of his left hand to his lips and leaning away):* Shhhh! The splashing has stopped. They may hear us.

El *(moving closer to the door without pressing her ear to it, in a whisper as Or):* No, I hear her giggling…. Him speaking.

Or *(straightening up):* Planting seeds of lascivious words in her ears.

El *(not changing her position):* To come up as screaming babies out of her womb.

Or *(louder, seething with anger, shaking the sword in his upraised hand):* Usurpers of our rights, who'll laugh at our rags, sic dogs on us to tear our bodies.

El *(worried, pressing her ear to the crack in the door again):* Shhhh! Don't speak so loud. They may hear us. *(After a pause.)* They're all quiet now.

Or *(moving his head closer to El's, trying to listen):* Only the water splashes rhythmically.

El: As it did with our father.

Or: In that mad girl's arms.

El *(tearing herself away from the door, standing up straight, determined):* We must get ready! The time has come.

Or *(standing up as El, even more determined than she):* It's now!

Scene 2

At that instant Py comes out of the darkness between the columns, carrying something tied in a bundle. El sees him and turns to him. Or does the same. Py comes up the two.

El *(anxiously, in a whisper):* You're just in time. Have you got it?

The three huddle together by the door. Py spreads the bundle in his hands. It turns out to be a fisherman's net.

Py *(in the same kind of voice):* Yes. It's just the right kind. Here, take it. *(Gives the net to Or.)* Or *(examining the net as best he can in the darkness, in the same kind of whisper):* It's not too thick? Won't blunt the sword?
Py: No. It's meant for small fishes. Old too... frayed... torn in places.... The sword will easily cut through it.
El *(anxiously):* But they won't tear it?... Free themselves?
Py: No, it'd be too hard. It'd take too much time.
Or: I... the sword... won't give it to them.
(Brandishes the sword while pressing the net to his chest with the other hand.) See how eager it is to do its work? Like a horse dancing in one spot, ready to go... neighing and rearing up.... Two stabs and they're done.
El: Two won't be enough.   They'll need more.
Or *(louder, brandishing the sword still more):* They'll get more! Many more! One apiece will be for starters... to let their bodies taste the sword... its sharp flavor. Then they'll feast on it....   Have their

fill... till they throw up...the red vomit of their blood.
El *(pressing her index finger to her lips):* Shhhh!
Enough rejoicing! Don't celebrate before the time
has come. Act first!
Py *(emphatically, but still in a whisper):* Act, then
dance with joy. Go! Go! The time has nearly
passed you. Act now!
El: Let's go!

*Or quickly unwinds the net, gives one end of it to
El, holds on to the other, the two rush to the door
and hurl themselves against it, making its two
wings fly open wide with a loud crash. Py runs
after them, but stops in the doorway and remains
there, still as a statue, watching what is going on
inside.*

Scene 3

Py *(in a loud yet calm voice, staring straight ahead,
but turning his head right from time to time and
speaking to the audience over his shoulder on the
background of the screams and sounds of the
splashing of water coming from backstage):* Aeg
turns his head left. There's utter surprise on his
face. Incomprehension. He doesn't understand
what's happening. Cly's face is turned right. Her
eyes are huge. They're about to pop out of their
sockets. She knows what's happening. A second
more and she'll know who the young man is,
although the last time she saw him he was a little
boy. In a couple of steps El and Or are by the

bathtub. They toss the net over the couple. It covers them like a mother's loving body a child. Aeg tries to free himself. Tries to stand up. Or lifts the sword in both hands high   above his head. Plunges it down with all his might into Aeg's curving back. It sinks half in. Aeg gasps. Sinks down into the water. Or struggles to pull the sword out. Succeeds. Cly screams his name, Orrrr! Noooo! Now she knows who he is!   Aeg's body shields her. Or tries to find a spot where to strike. Pushes Aeg away with his foot. El helps him. She grabs Aeg's hair through the net. Pulls on it. Exposes Cly's face and chest. Cly screams, Orrrr! Ellll! Noooo! Noooo! Noooo! Or plunges the sword into her mouth. It comes out easily. Or stabs Cly over and over again. In her neck, chest. Aeg stirs. Tries to get up. Or plunges his sword into his neck. Then the back. Over and over again. He's spluttered with blood. There's blood everywhere. The bathtub is a cauldron of boiling blood. The floor around it is covered with a tattered blood rug. There're fancy blood tapestries on the gray granite walls. Or turns around. His eyes are two flaming torches. His sword falls limp out of his hand. Something huge and heavy has found its way into his arms. He can barely hold it. Barely shuffles along. Reels. A soft whine like a thin stream of steam escapes from his mouth.   El follows a few steps behind him, watching his progress. There's profound surprise on her face. She didn't expect this. None of us did.

Py steps out of the doorway, making room for the two to pass, then turns right and follows them with his eyes.

Scene 4

Out of the doorway comes Or, followed by El a few steps behind him, both covered head to toe with blood. He carries a huge blood-smeared boulder in his arms, pressing it with all his strength to his chest. The rock threatens to slip out of his hands any minute and come crashing down to the floor, crushing his feet. He staggers forward, however, with his knees bent, reeling from side to side. His face is red from the strain and eyes bulge out of their sockets. After a few steps El comes up to him and lifts her arm, as if wanting to put her hand on his shoulder in order to help him. He indicates by shaking his head for her to leave him alone, however. In the meantime Py has also come up to Or, obviously with the same intention as El, but seeing Or's reaction to El's offer, doesn't raise his arm. The two stay behind Or, as if his double shadow, slowly moving along.

Or *(haltingly, in a strained, compressed voice):* A, a, a, a, a…. A, a, a, a, a…. Killer of his own mother…. A, a, a, a, a…. Avenger of his father's death…. A, a, a, a, a…. Murderer…. A, a, a, a, a…. Avenger murderer…. Who will forgive me?... Who'll punish me to ease my guilt?

*He reaches the edge of the stage, falls down on his
knees, and tries to roll over onto his back while
continuing to clutch the boulder. El and Py bend
down and help him, making sure the rock doesn't
slip out of his hands. Or tires to find the right
position on the floor, achieves this, El and Py help
him place the rock on his chest and stand up.*

Or *(walking as before, barely able to speak, his
voice practically mere   air escaping out of his
chest):* Where will I find peace?... Where will I find
a place where I'm not myself?... Aaa...aaa... aaa...
aaaaa....

*El and Py stand still, bending over Or, their faces
blank with pain at being unable to help him.*

*3.2.2 Rewrite the play developed in 3.1.3.3,
changing as many of its elements as desired,
without affecting the basic story to create a
different but effective impact on the viewer.*

Comment: Rewriting the description, Scene 2, and
Scene 3 in a contemporary manner.

The Avengers
(Contemporary Version)

*A long narrow corridor with an extremely high
ceiling, brightly illuminated with an unpleasant
white neon light, lined on both sides with floor-to-
ceiling bookcases crammed full with books, for the*

most part placed helter-skelter. A tiny door at the end of it, big enough for a dog or a child but definitely not for an adult. The door shut. A two-winged, narrow but likewise extremely tall (also ceiling-high) white door up front, house right. This door also shut.

The three characters—El, Or, and Py—young, pale, frail-looking, with sunken chests, thin limbs, pale complexion, and short blond hair. El (female) dressed in a long, loose, shapeless dress with sleeves, made out of a thin, sleazy, faded blue-gray fabric. Or and Py (both male) dressed in long-sleeved shirts made out of the same fabric as El's dress, and pants from a stiff material of the same color. Some buttons missing on Or's shirt, in particular on the cuff of his right sleeve, which flaps around as he moves his arm. All three characters barefoot. In spite of the difference in gender, the three looking like identical triplets. Or carries a long, shiny rapier in his hand.

Scene 1

El and Or hunched over, huddling against the door.

El *(in a half-whisper, pressing her ear to the crack in the door):* Is that water I hear splashing?
Or *(also in a half-whisper, moving his head close to that of El while staying by the door):* The quiet waters of the Styx roiled up by our hatred.

Both continuing speaking in the same manner, their bodies glued to the door.

El: That will come later. Now it's the warm arms of the bath lulling them into half-sleep, to ease our task. *(Leans away from the door.)*
Or *(pressing his ear to the crack now)*: Our accomplice, fourth co-conspirator.
El: It was their third one eight years ago.
Or: Yes, it put its soft palms tightly over our father's eyes.
El *(angry):* Monstrous nature, evil villain, helping out where it can to see us writhe in pain at its feet, no matter who we are.
Or *(in a whisper, pressing the index finger of his left hand to his lips and leaning away):*   Shhhh! The splashing has stopped.   They may hear us.
El *(moving closer to the door without pressing her ear to it, in a whisper as Or):* No, I hear her giggling.... Him speaking.
Or *(straightening up):* Planting seeds of lascivious words in her ears.
El *(not changing her position):* To come up as screaming babies out of her womb.
Or *(louder, seething with anger, shaking the sword in his upraised hand):* Usurpers of our rights, who'll laugh at our rags, sic dogs on us to tear our bodies.
El *(worried, pressing her ear to the crack in the door again):* Shhhh! Don't speak so loud. They may hear us. *(After a pause.)* They're all quiet now.
Or *(moving his head closer to El's, trying to listen):* Only the water splashes rhythmically.

El: As it did with our father.

Or: In that mad girl's arms.

El *(tearing herself away from the door, standing up straight, determined):* We must get ready! The time has come.

Or *(standing up as El, even more determined than she):* It's now!

Scene 2

At that instant Py appears at the end of the corridor, obviously not from the tiny door but from somewhere on the left. There must be another door there between the bookcases which cannot be seen by the audience. He carries a big piece of cloth of the same color as his shirt and pants, tied into a bundle, which he presses to his chest. It is wet and drips water. El sees Py and turns to him. Or does the same. Py comes up to the two.

El *(anxiously, in a whisper):* You're just in time. Have you got it?

The three huddle together by the door. Py spreads the bundle in his hands.

Py *(in the same kind of voice):* I couldn't get a net but I got something better... a sheet.... I soaked it in water and it's heavy. It'll cover them real well and they won't' be able to see from under it. Here, take it. *(Gives the bundle to Or.)*

Or *(examining the sheet, in the same kind of*

whisper): The sword will cut through it? It won't blunt it?

Py: No. It's thin... like your shirt.

El *(anxiously):* But they won't be able to tear it?... Free themselves?

Py: No, it's too strong. It'd be too hard.... Would take too much time.

Or: I... the sword... won't give it to them. *(Brandishes the sword while pressing the sheet to his chest with the other hand.)* See how eager it is to do its work? Like a horse dancing in one spot, ready to go... neighing and rearing up.... Two stabs and they're done.

El: Two won't be enough. They'll need more.

Or *(louder, brandishing the sword still more):* They'll get more! Many more! One apiece will be for starters... to let their bodies taste the sword... its sharp flavor. Then they'll feast on it.... Have their fill... till they throw up... the red vomit of their blood.

El *(pressing her index finger to her lips):* Shhhh! Enough rejoicing! Don't celebrate before the time has come. Act first!

Py *(emphatically, but still in a whisper):* Act, then dance with joy.   Go! Go! The time has nearly passed you. Act now!

El: Let's go!

Or quickly spreads the sheet, gives one end of it to El, holds on to the other, the two rush to the door and hurl themselves against it, making its two wings fly open wide with a loud crash. Py runs after them, but stops in the doorway and remains there, still as a statue, watching what is going on inside.

Scene 3

Py *(in a loud yet calm voice, staring straight ahead, but turning his head right from time to time and speaking to the audience over his shoulder on the background of screams and sounds of the splashing of water coming from backstage):* Aeg turns his head left. There's utter surprise on his face. Incomprehension. He doesn't understand what's happening. Cly's face is turned right. Her eyes are huge. They're about to pop out of their sockets. She knows what's happening. A second more and she'll know who the young man is, although the last time she saw him he was a little boy. In a couple of steps El and Or are by the bathtub. They toss the sheet over the couple. It covers them like a mother's loving body a child. Aeg tries to free himself. Tries to stand up. Or lifts the sword in both hands high above his head. Plunges it down with all his might into Aeg's curving back. It sinks half in. Aeg gasps. Sinks down into the water. Or struggles to pull the sword out. Succeeds. Cly screams his name, Orrrr! Noooo! Now she knows who he is! Aeg's body shields her. Or tries to find a spot where to strike. Pushes Aeg away with his foot. El helps him. She grabs Aeg's head through the sheet. Pulls on it. Exposes Cly's face and chest. Cly screams, Orrrr! Ellll! Noooo! Noooo! Noooo! Or plunges the sword into her face...

mouth. It comes out easily. Or stabs Cly over and over again. In her neck, chest. Aeg stirs. Tries to get up. Or plunges his sword into his neck. Then the back. Over and over again. He's spluttered with blood. There's blood everywhere. The bathtub is a cauldron of boiling blood. The floor around it is covered with a tattered blood rug. There're thin, tattered rags of blood all over on the white tiled walls. Or turns around. His eyes are two flaming torches. His sword falls limp out of his hand. He stumbles forward. Reels from side to side as he walks. A soft whine like a thin stream of steam escapes from his mouth. El follows a few steps behind him, watching his progress. There's profound surprise on her face. She didn't expect this. None of us did.

Py steps out of the doorway, making room for the two to pass, then turns right and follows them with his eyes.

Scene 4

Out of the doorway comes Or, followed by El a few steps behind him, both covered head to toe with blood. Or moves slowly forward, pushing his feet on the floor without lifting them like a blind man afraid to fall down. His arms hang limp along his sides and his face is blank.

Or *(without emotion, barely audibly):*
Aaaaaaaaaaaaaaaa….   Aaaaaaaaaaaaaaaa….

Aaaaaaaaaaaaaaaa…. Killer of his own mother….
Aaaaaaaaaaaaaaaa…. Avenger of his father's
death…. Aaaaaaaaaaaaaaaa…. Murderer….
Aaaaaaaaaaaaaaaa…. Avenger murderer…. Who
will forgive me?... Who'll punish me to ease my
guilt?... Aaaaaaaaaaaaaaaa…. Where will I find
peace?... Where will I find a place where I'm not
myself?... Aaaaaaaaaaaaaaaaaaaaaaaaaaaaa….

*He reaches the edge of the stage, falls down on his
knees, and collapses with his face on the floor and
arms thrown out before him. El falls on her knees a
few feet behind and to the side of him and stares
vacant-eyed at his prostrate body. Py watches the
two from the distance, an expression of
helplessness on his face.*

*Compare the three versions. What conclusions can
you draw from the differences between them?*

The original version of the play of 3.1.3.3 is placed
in a coarse, archaic, "Neanderthal" setting, which is
appropriate for the brutal story—one isn't surprised
too much by people from those times acting in such
a fashion.

The "metaphorical" behavior of the character Or in
Scene 4 of the "nonrealistic" version of 3.2.1 not
only fits in well in the given situation but actually
strengthens it—it introduces a new stone element
into a setting already filled with stones (the stage
crowded with the thick granite columns and the

stone-age characters) and the character's behavior isn't all that surprising for someone from that period; it certainly would seem more unusual for a person from our age. This version, therefore, may be considered to be an improvement over the original one.

The narrow corridor lined with bookcases and especially the tiny useless door at its end in the "contemporary" version of 3.2.2 create an atmosphere similar to that in Sartre's play *Huis clos [No Exit]*—the only way out for the characters on the stage is through the door on the right, which implies the bloody act that would follow. This is supported by the appearance of the three characters who look like stereotypical existentialists of the classical existentialism times—pale-complexioned and frail-bodied intellectuals who spend their times in coffee houses and among books. Here the character Or's behavior in Scene 4, which is unchanged from the original version, is very much in line with his appearance; it may seem to be too "modern" for a Neanderthal character in the version of 3.1.3.3. This third version of the play may appeal more to some viewers, first, because of creating a tension between the contemporary setting and the archaic-sounding spoken text, and second, because of stressing the universal nature of the tragic situation by bringing it to our times.

The identical triplets similarity between the three

characters in all three versions stresses their emotional and physical involvement in the plot. They act as one person.

Comment: The fourth variant of the play, which corresponds to a nonrealistic rendering of the contemporary version and which rounds off the drama exercise, may be found under the title "The Revenge" in Yuriy Tarnawsky, *Crocodile Smiles*, Black *Scat Books,* 2014. The reason for selecting an existing title for a new work was partly to show that this could be done without causing any lasting harm, and partly, an attempt to illustrate the impact a title may have on a literary work—it was the title from which grew the story of the novel.

Repeat these exercises a few times.

Exercise skipped.

Yuriy Tarnawsky has authored some three dozen books of poetry, fiction, drama, essays, and translations in English and Ukrainian, including the novels *Meningitis* and *Three Blondes and Death*, the collections of short stories *Short Tails* and *Crocodile Smiles*, three collections of mininovels *Like Blood in Water, The Future of Giraffes*, and *View of Delft* comprising *The Placebo Effect Trilogy*, a collection of *Heuristic* poetry *Modus Tollens*, and the book of essays *Claim to Oblivion*. He was born in Ukraine but was raised and educated in the West. An engineer and linguist by training, he has worked as computer scientist specializing in Artificial Intelligence at IBM Corporation and professor of Ukrainian literature and culture at Columbia University. He resides with his wife Karina in the New York City metropolitan area.

***

Struggling with your iambs and pentameters? Characters and plots? Have you hit the concrete wall of a writer's block? Or are you having the time of your life seeing your pen trace out graceful meanders of words on the blank pages before you or your fleet fingers make letters dutifully jump off the keyboard of your laptop onto the screen above it? Whichever is the case, you must try these 100 exercises the artist and educator in Yuriy Tarnawsky have conjured up for you. What the gentle stretching on the yoga mat does for your muscles and joints, these painful tasks will do for the writing talents inside you. You may return to them again, and again, and again.

A checklist of JEF titles

90252767R00147

Made in the USA
Lexington, KY
10 June 2018